M000286288

SCOTT DELUZIO

Surviving Son

An Afghanistan War Veteran Reveals His Nightmare Of
Becoming A Gold Star Brother

First published by Drive On Studio, LLC 2021

Copyright © 2021 by Scott DeLuzio

All rights reserved. No part of this publication may be reproduced, stored or transmitted in any form or by any means, electronic, mechanical, photocopying, recording, scanning, or otherwise without written permission from the publisher. It is illegal to copy this book, post it to a website, or distribute it by any other means without permission.

Scott DeLuzio has no responsibility for the persistence or accuracy of URLs for external or third-party Internet Websites referred to in this publication and does not guarantee that any content on such Websites is, or will remain, accurate or appropriate.

Scott DeLuzio is not a mental health professional and has not written this book intending to replace the advice of mental health professionals. The events written about in this book are from Scott's memories and his perspective. He has tried to represent these events as accurately as possible. In certain circumstances, he relied on the accounts of others to fill in details of these events he was unable to obtain on his own. To maintain the anonymity of certain individuals, he has omitted or changed the names used in the book. The appearance of U.S. Department of Defense (DoD) visual information does not imply or constitute DoD endorsement.

Cover Photography by Candace Weir

First edition

ISBN: 978-0-578-97744-7

This book was professionally typeset on Reedsy.
Find out more at reedsy.com

Contents

Preface   iv

Acknowledgement   vii

Praise for Surviving Son   viii

1   Early Years   1

2   Call To Service   11

3   Family and Country   33

4   Afghanistan   43

5   August 22, 2010   56

6   The Homecoming   75

7   Return To Civilian Life   88

8   Family Life   99

9   Mental Health   109

10 Looking Forward   117

Afterword   130

Pictures   132

Resources   169

Glossary   172

Index   181

About the Author   195

Preface

"DELUZIO!" I HEAR from the mental health counselor calling down the hall. My name was the next on the list of soldiers from the Connecticut Army National Guard's 1/102nd Infantry Regiment. Since we recently returned from Afghanistan, we all had to attend mandatory mental health screenings. I got up out of my chair and started walking towards the voice that called my name. I pass a few of my friends, who were also waiting their turn. I roll my eyes as if to say, "I can't wait for this to be over."

When I enter the room, the counselor closes the door behind me and asks me to sit down. He starts asking me questions about our deployment to Afghanistan. He asks about things like trauma and death. Those are things you would expect a mental health counselor to ask if you had recently deployed. He also asks about habits and routines at home now that we've returned. The entire time I keep thinking to myself, "just say what he wants to hear so I can get out of here as fast as possible." Check the box, and move on. If you have deployed, you might have even done the same thing.

It shouldn't come as a surprise that I felt that way about speaking to the mental health counselors. The Army paraded me in and out of these offices in the months after returning from Afghanistan. Every time I had the same attitude. Answer their questions with what they want to hear so that they let me go as soon as possible. One time, I remember the counselor asking me about my drinking habits, and I slipped up by telling the truth.

"That's an awful lot to be drinking," the counselor said. "Do you feel that it is hurting your work or personal relationships?" Thinking quickly, I said, "Oh, no, work is fine. My relationships are great. I thought you were talking about recently, and we had a party that might have gone a little overboard, but I don't make it a habit." Satisfying the checklist requirements he was working from allowed me to skate by without any further questioning.

Looking back, I wish I was more honest during those mental health screenings. It may have saved me from years of struggling with PTSD and depression. I likely wouldn't have had to rely on alcohol and sleeping pills to get to sleep. Those mental health screenings would have allowed me to learn how to deal with the emotions I was experiencing. At least, in a healthier way than how I ended up dealing with them. It may have allowed me to have lived life in the moment instead of in the past.

When you have PTSD, your reality can get skewed. This distorted view of the world can cause problems in social and work environments. It can create problems in your relationships with your family, friends, neighbors, and co-workers. If you suffer from PTSD, you may experience intrusive memories like having flashbacks of the traumatic event. You might avoid places or activities that remind you of the traumatic event. You might experience negative thoughts and moods where you feel emotionally numb or have no interest in doing things you once enjoyed. Maybe you even become easily startled, hyper-vigilant, or display self-destructive behavior like drinking too much.

In some cases, like mine, you will experience all of those adverse effects.

This book is my story of the obstacles I faced during my military career as an Army infantryman. It talks about the pain of losing a loved one and what I experienced after I got out of the military.

I'm writing this book for several reasons. First, like veterans of other wars, I am writing it so that people don't forget the sacrifices made by the soldiers sent overseas to defend our country. Without books like theirs, and this one, we may soon forget about the individuals who we, as a nation, sent off to war. Even if you are a veteran, each of our stories is unique. I can benefit from hearing your story, and I hope that you will benefit from hearing mine.

Additionally, I want my children to have something to read when they are old enough to be interested in my and their Uncle Steven's military service. More than just my family, though, it is vital for you and future generations to understand the past and learn its lessons.

Finally, I am writing it hoping that some of the things I went through can help you, whether you are a civilian, veteran, or a part of a military family. Sometimes knowing that you're not alone is all we need.

This book contains a true story, written with countless hours of research. However, some names have been changed or withheld throughout the book to protect operational security and privacy.

While I've written about death, grief, and mental health, I am not a mental health professional. None of the things I write about in this book substitute for advice from a mental health professional. I am sharing these topics hoping that you can learn from my mistakes and not make the same mistakes in your own life or in the lives of those you love.

Acknowledgement

WRITING A BOOK about a deeply personal topic is incredibly difficult. It is a lot of work to get the book written. It is also emotionally draining to relive certain experiences discussed in the book. Without an incredible support network, I don't know that I could have finished this book.

I have to start by thanking my incredible wife, Vicki. She played a key role in getting this book across the finish line from reading early drafts, providing advice on the cover, and giving me time to write. Also, for sticking with me when I was at my worst. Thank you so much!

A special thanks to my parents, Mark and Diane, who raised me to be a patriotic American. They instilled the values of God, Family, and Country in me at an early age, and I hope that I am doing a good job passing those values to my children. Those values enabled me to be the type of person who stepped up when our country needed me. Also, thank you for all of your support with this book. Everything from reading the draft copy to your content and editorial suggestions helped make this book a reality.

Praise for Surviving Son

Scott successfully captured the unique perspectives of both Soldier and Family from an angle few will ever know. His ability to help us feel his story physically, emotionally, and patriotically makes one appreciate the sacrifices of our Citizen Soldiers and the cost of freedom.

    - COL (R) Rob Salome – Combat Infantryman, Iraq & Afghanistan, USMA '94

Warriors share stories to impart lessons to the next generation, to inspire those around them, and to keep alive the memories of their fallen brothers and sisters. Scott had the courage to write these words, but this story belongs to a generation of heroes.

    - LTC (R) Mike P. Maloney, United States Army Special Forces

Scott's heavy-hitting story should be an amazing example to all about the true heroes that make up our armed forces. His story of courage, sacrifice and hope despite losing his brother is more important than ever given the failed withdrawal of Afghanistan. I highly encourage you to read this amazing story. Men like Scott and his brother are what make it possible for us all to live the American Dream.

    - LT Edward Crawford, Navy Intelligence Officer –SOTF-SE Afghanistan and Bronze Star Recipient

Surviving Son is a raw and personal testimony of what freedom looks like. The sacrifices, losses, and bravery that looks far beyond signing the dotted line on a contract to serve our great United States of America.

    - Ashlee Leppert, US Coast Guard Air Medal recipient, and author of The Hurricane Within

As I read through Scott's book it opened up some old wounds of my own. Scott has brought to light and truly captures the anguish that too many have lived through. Gaining an insight and understanding to his loss is unique and worthy of reading.

- John McLellan (Doc Mac) HM1 FMF (8404) USN/USNR 1981-2002

If you have the pleasure of reading Scott's accurate, heartfelt account of what it's really like to have been a warrior in Afghanistan - only to lose his brother as they both fought valiantly for our freedoms mere miles from each other - you'll come away with the truth about this war at such a crucial time as this... *Surviving Son* is a must-read!

- Jennifer O'Neill, Actress/ Author/ Speaker, and Founder of Hope & Healing at Hillenglade

Scott DeLuzio is raw and honest about the trauma of losing his brother who was killed in combat. By sharing his journey through grief, Scott helps others know how to reconstruct a life shattered by loss.

- Dr. Sherry Walling, clinical psychologist, author of The Entrepreneur's Guide to Keeping Your Sh*t Together, *and host of the* Zenfounder *podcast*

1

Early Years

THE EARLY EXPERIENCES IN MY LIFE helped to shape who I am today. Those experiences ultimately had a direct impact on the decisions I made in life. I want to reflect on my early life in this book, so the reader understands who I was before becoming a soldier.

In WWII, my paternal grandfather, Alfred DeLuzio, served in the US Navy on the destroyer USS Boyd. Among the battles he participated, were the liberation of the Philippines and Iwo Jima. Unfortunately, I don't know much about his Navy service since I was pretty young when he passed away. Every time he would start talking about the war, my grandmother would smack him and say, "Fred, stop talking about that God damn Navy."

One of the reasons I am writing this book is so future generations can learn what it was like to be in the military in the post-9/11 era.

Joseph Lysik, my maternal grandfather, grew up in Poland and lived through the Nazi occupation during WWII. He survived the war as a civilian but didn't escape Nazi terror. The Nazis captured him and others from his town in Poland and brought them to Germany. He spent some time living on a farm owned by a Nazi. At one point during his time there, he attempted to escape. When he got caught, his Nazi captor beat him unconscious. He was then chained in a barn and forced to work while living in conditions unfit for even an animal. He didn't talk about his time at the farm with me, but my mother told me stories she heard from him. In one of these stories, American soldiers freed him. After the liberation, a US soldier handed my grandfather a pistol and told him to kill his former captor. According to the story, despite the harsh treatment, he couldn't bring himself to kill him. After the war, he fled Europe for the safety of American shores and the hope to live the American dream.

My parents were born in 1956. Both of my parents grew up with a parent who likely had PTSD from their experiences during WWII. However, the term PTSD wasn't in use back then. A psychologist might have diagnosed them with "Shell Shock" or "Battle Fatigue" if they ever sought treatment. As far as I know, they didn't. That wasn't something many people would do back then. While my grandparents may have seen the terror that war can bring firsthand, my parents only saw what the nightly news would show. My dad remembers watching the news during the Vietnam War with great interest. He missed getting called up for the Vietnam draft by only one year, but he knew plenty of people who served in that war. He would watch the body count ticker on the news as body bags would arrive back home by the hundreds almost daily.

I grew up during a relatively peaceful time in our country. I was born in 1982, two years after my parents married, and I was a pain in the ass from day one. My mom often reminds me of my birth weight, 10 pounds 9.5 ounces, when I've been a pain to her. My mom never forgot that extra half ounce, so she got credit for pushing out a child the size of a bowling ball. My younger brother Steven came along about a month before my third birthday.

As kids, my dad would take us out in the backyard and teach us how to play baseball and golf. When Steven was only two years old, my dad brought us out to the backyard. That day, he taught me how to hit a baseball, which I was doing pretty well with the kid-sized wooden bat he got me. Everything was going great until Steven chased a beach ball that blew directly behind me. My dad taught me to keep my eye on the ball as I was swinging, which I obediently did. Unfortunately, as good as his coaching and my mechanics were, my bat never contacted the ball. Steven's forehead abruptly stopped the bat as he stepped into my backswing.

"Remember to check behind you before you swing so you don't hit Steven," my dad's warning echoed in my head.

We rushed Steven to the emergency room, with blood pouring down his face, to get him fixed up. Several painful stitches and a lot of agonizing screaming later, he was good as new. Well, almost as good as new. He probably had a wicked headache and developed a nasty scar right in the center of his forehead, which never really went away. He never held a grudge about it, though, or if he did, he never said anything about it to me.

My parents, who lived through much of the Cold War, would remind us that evil exists in the world. They would also remind us that we should be thankful for those willing to fight to keep us safe. This reminder helped instill pride in America and our nation's military in my brother and me.

When Steven and I were kids, my parents took us on vacation to Southern California. There, we hit all the fun tourist stops like Disneyland and SeaWorld. One day on that trip, my dad decided to take us down to Tijuana, Mexico. He took us there to show us how lucky we were to grow up in America. He showed us how even just a short distance across an international border could drastically change the quality of life the people experienced. Vendors approached us, selling everything from candy to scavenged animal bones. One vendor came to Steven trying to sell him a cow's skull for $25. Steven fired back, "No, dos dolares" (two dollars) in his best elementary school level Spanish. The man was offended that Steven would make such a low offer that he moved on to the next group of Americans.

The trip emphasized to us how good we have it back home in America. It made us appreciate the quality of life we enjoy even more than we already did. Most importantly, though, it instilled a sense of pride in our country. To us, America was something special.

As kids, my brother and I loved the made-for-television version of the movie Top Gun. Our infatuation wasn't because we liked planes or missiles, although that didn't hurt. Instead, we looked up to the actor's portrayal of the military we learned to respect. We would pretend we were in dogfights by sticking a wooden spoon between the couch cushions for our "plane's" flight controls. We would act like we were emergency ejecting into a pile of pillows on the floor when we got knocked out of the sky.

3

In the early 1990s, my parents took us up to Westover Air Reserve Base in Massachusetts to greet the soldiers returning from Operation Desert Storm. Steven and I got all decked out in our junior camouflage uniforms that my mom bought for us. To us, it was almost like meeting a celebrity, except we didn't know any of the soldiers' names. As a young kid, the war was fascinating to me. Watching the nightly news show footage through a night vision lens with green streaks of light flashing across the screen was thrilling. I tried to learn everything I could about what was happening in the war. When I was about eight years old, my mom helped me put together a scrapbook with newspaper clippings that described the military weapons used in the Gulf War. I still have that scrapbook to this day.

Our parents taught us to respect the flag and taught us how to recite the national anthem and pledge of allegiance by heart. We even have an old home movie of Steven and me standing in our front yard with me holding an American flag as he sings the national anthem.

Besides our fascination with the military and our love for our country, my brother and I grew up as two regular suburban kids. We both played baseball, hockey, and later learned to golf. We rode bikes, climbed trees, and all the other things you would expect of two upper-middle-class kids.

Jumping ahead a few years, I have fond memories of the hell we'd raise when Steven and I got season tickets to the Boston Bruins. One game we went to see in Boston was against the Montreal Canadiens. The Bruins pulled out a win, and it created a whole "USA is better than Canada" vibe in the arena as we were walking out. Steven and I both had a few beers, so we were loud, rowdy, and I'd imagine a little obnoxious too. With wall-to-wall people, Steven starts chanting "USA, USA, USA." This chant got thousands of Bostonians to begin a loud "USA" chant in the halls exiting the arena. It was a glorious experience. After we finally left the arena, we were starving because all we put in our mouths for the last few hours was beer. We found a burger place nearby, and we sat down to order our meals. While we ordered, we were still excited about the "USA" chant and the great game we had watched. When Steven gave his order, the waiter asked if Canadian bacon was okay on his burger. Steven's smile turned serious in an instant as if the waiter had insulted him. Steven

4

looked the waiter in the eye and said, "Hell no, I don't want Canadian bacon. I want AMERICAN bacon!" The waiter laughed as Steven's smile returned. The waiter then asked if he wanted french fries on the side. Steven's smile faded again much the same way as it did before as he said, "Fuck no, I want AMERICAN fries!" The rest of the night is a blur, but that was the kind of guy he was.

He was also fiercely competitive and enjoyed anything that had a winner and a loser. Steven loved competition, whether it was the Yankees, the Bruins, or a ping pong match with friends. He'd watch ESPN's SportsCenter daily and even began to talk like the reporters. Steven would rattle off statistics about players that most casual fans never even knew. Steve's circle of friends knew that he was the best source for scores, standings, and schedules before the Internet and smartphones.

Once, my dad and Steven were playing basketball in our driveway, and Steven started getting a little too competitive. Since he was a hockey player, he lowered his shoulder into my dad's chest as he prepared to take a shot. The move wouldn't have looked out of place on the ice, but in our driveway, playing basketball, it was a bit much. After they made contact, the wind got knocked out of my dad. Not only that, Steven's hit was so hard that he cracked several of my dad's ribs.

My dad was supposed to play golf with several colleagues later that week, and with this injury, he wasn't sure if he would be able to play. Eventually, he decided he would play, even though each stroke was rather painful. During that round, my dad scored his first eagle (2 under par) ever. I don't know if that is a testament to my dad's resilience or if his golf game was just so bad that he needed a broken rib to straighten out his game! Either way, it's a story my dad still tells to this day.

He also had a great sense of humor and was a big goofball. If you were having a bad day, Steven would find a way to make you laugh, even if his persistence was somewhat annoying. To get a laugh, he used to pretend to fall asleep during conversations that he found boring. It didn't matter if he was standing up or sitting down. Steven would always end up on the floor fake-snoring.

He was also a natural-born leader. In high school, his class elected him to be the class president. In 2003, the year he was a co-captain of the school's hockey team, his leadership helped lead the team to win the state championship. That was a challenging year for his class as three of their classmates died in a car crash, so the team needed strong leadership to get through the remainder of the season. His coach later said that he believed that Steven's leadership is what won them the championship.

When we were younger, you might have guessed we would get white-collar nine-to-five jobs when we grew up. Since Steven and I both earned degrees in accounting, you wouldn't have been wrong.

His path was different than mine, though. Following his freshman year at Hofstra University, Steven decided he needed to become more disciplined. He found himself partying more than studying, and his grades reflected that. Steven told us that he wanted to join the military to get the discipline he was lacking. My parents were concerned that he wouldn't finish college if he dropped out and joined the military. They had nothing against him joining the military, but they knew the importance of a college degree.

My father had an acquaintance who attended Norwich University, a military college in Vermont, so he called him for advice. Norwich was the country's first private military college and home to the ROTC (Reserve Officer Training Corps). Besides the traditional educational programs, my father learned about the Corps of Cadets. He then put Steven in touch with this acquaintance, where Steven found out that the Corps of Cadets will prepare you for military service if you choose to go that route. While many people go on to join the military after graduation, it is not a requirement. It seemed like the perfect fit for Steven, as it offered him the rigorous lifestyle he desired and a quality education. My parents' minds were at ease since he would be able to finish his education before joining the military.

Steven applied and got accepted to Norwich University for the 2004 fall semester. Despite this being his second year of college, he was still a "rook," or a first-year cadet for training purposes. Before classes began, he had to go through a 10-day "Rook Orientation." There he got issued uniforms while learning Norwich's traditions and military etiquette. There are also several physically demanding events, including the Dog River Run. Despite the short distance, the one-mile run ends in a way that allows the rooks to understand the unity that comes from shared suffering.

Steven went through "Rook Basic Skills Training" during his first few months at Norwich. During this time, he got removed from society except for a few five-minute calls home. We were eager to drive up for his first family weekend towards the middle of the first semester because he hadn't been able to speak to us much. During this visit, Steven told us that he intended to join the Vermont National Guard. One of his friends at the school was already in a nearby infantry unit, and the more Steven learned about it, the more attractive it became. My parents couldn't believe what they were hearing. Their baby, who led his high school hockey team two years earlier to become state champions, wanted to join the military! Steven joining the military before graduation was not what my parents hoped for when he transferred to Norwich.

Steven had made up his mind. According to him, as long as he remained in school, he would not get deployed to Iraq or Afghanistan. So, in October 2004, he enlisted in the Vermont Army National Guard as a part of A Company 3/172 Infantry Regiment. My parents were concerned with Steven joining the military during wartime. Yet, they were still proud of him for doing so.

Steven found his grades improved a bit during his first year at Norwich, although not drastically. He was enjoying this new lifestyle, though. He had a much different experience at Norwich than he did partying at college the previous year. It appeared that Norwich planned each day to set the cadets up for success. According to Norwich University, a day in the life of a cadet consists of:

- 5:30 am: First Call – at least three days a week, physical fitness training (PT) gets conducted in the morning
- 7:30 – 8 am: Breakfast
- 8 am – 4 pm: Academic Day
- 11:30 am – 1 pm: Lunch
- 4 – 6 pm: Extracurricular Activities (athletics, club activities, etc.)

- 5 – 7 pm: Dinner
- 6:30 – 7 pm: Commanders' Time – Reserved for extra Corps training
- 7:30 – 11 pm: Mandatory Study Hall
- 11 pm: Lights Out

After his first year at Norwich, Steven attended basic training and advanced individual training (AIT) at Ft. Benning, GA. Whatever his time at Norwich failed to provide in military training, he learned at basic training. Steven quickly learned how challenging the military could be. Additionally, we learned from him how difficult it was when the drill sergeants allowed him to call home for a few minutes at a time. After those few short minutes, in the background, you could hear the drill sergeant yelling at him to hang up.

During that three-and-a-half-month period, he wrote to us more often than he called. Steven wrote about achieving new training milestones, which was great to see. The days began early and ended late, with PT, quick meals, marksmanship training, and combat maneuvers, among other things. We sent plenty of letters, which helped fill the void. He wasn't allowed to receive newspapers or even clippings from the paper, so my mom would include highlights from recent Yankees games in her letters. It wasn't much, but it was all we could do for moral support.

Between Basic Training and Advanced Individual Training, Steven's company got a 36-hour leave from Ft. Benning. My parents and I went down for a visit, along with Steven's girlfriend, Leeza. Steven was glad to get his first whole night's sleep in weeks at the hotel with us. He slept in late, so we were a little antsy for him to wake up. Upon returning to the room, we opened the curtains to let in the sunlight. Steven jumped out of bed, almost hitting his head on the ceiling. It was funny to watch his utter confusion and panic as he assessed the unfamiliar surroundings. Luckily for him, it was only us and not a drill sergeant yelling at him for sleeping in late. The rest of the weekend together was enjoyable and a much-needed distraction for Steven.

After finishing his training at Ft. Benning, Steven returned home as a full-fledged US Army infantryman. As I recall, he seemed to be even more fit and confident about tackling whatever obstacles came his way. Steven even received the Cadet of the Month award for the best performance on various PT exercises the first month back at Norwich after Basic Training.

I was so proud of all that he had done. I raved about him to my friends, co-workers, and even some random person at a bar once. My brother was now one of those guys I had idolized at Westover Air Reserve Base almost 15 years earlier.

As he returned to Vermont, he joined his unit and attended classes at Norwich for his junior year. He enjoyed having a bit more freedom than he had the year before since he was no longer a "rook." Since joining the National Guard, the school let him keep his car on campus. That way, if he ever had to respond to a state emergency, he would have transportation available. Not every cadet gets this privilege as early as he did.

In late 2005, Steven volunteered for deployment to Iraq. He was training with the rear detachment for a unit already in Ramadi in the Al Anbar Province in Western Iraq. They needed reinforcements due to losses sustained in battle. He volunteered to support them in the last six months of their 18-month deployment, waiving his non-deployable status.

Looking back now, I don't know whether the "non-deployable" status was true or a white lie he used to soften his decision to join the Army for our parents. Knowing what I know now, the Army doesn't give you too many choices about when or where you will get deployed. He did tell us that he volunteered for this deployment with about 20 other soldiers.

News of his deployment shocked me because I had counted on the "protection" being a student at Norwich offered. That's not to say that I wasn't very proud of him for volunteering. It just caught me off guard.

Soldiers in the early to mid-2000s expected that an infantryman would get deployed at some point. His deployment couldn't have come as much of a surprise to him. He may have even wanted to deploy to get the inevitable out of the way.

I accepted that it was out of my hands, and I couldn't protect him in this situation. Not being able to defend him was strange because, as the bigger brother, I always took on the role of the protector with him. I did not let myself get worried about what could happen to him because I couldn't prevent it no matter what I did. Like me, my dad felt a sense of patriotic pride that Steven would be serving his country. However, my mom's natural motherly worries went into overdrive. In what seemed like an overnight transition, she had gone from chasing after us with sunscreen to thinking, "My son is heading for a combat zone." The other thing weighing on my parents is that I had also chosen to enlist and would soon be leaving for basic training (more on that later).

In the weeks before he left, Steven's grades dropped even more, so it's clear that he was worried about his deployment. He found his professors to be understanding and lenient when it came to makeup exams and late papers. They were supportive of him and the situation he was in with his upcoming deployment.

Steven was also involved in a scary car accident. In hindsight, the accident is pretty funny. Since he had spent the past year in Vermont, he knew that the winters were snowy and icy. However, one day, while slowly driving from Norwich to his unit's armory on slick roads, he encountered a particularly icy spot. His car started to skid on some ice and ended up doing a 180-degree turn in the middle of the highway. As Steven sat there trying to figure out how to turn around and get back on the road, a second car traveling in the same direction slammed head-on into his vehicle.

Steven looked at the car that hit him and saw nothing but a big red splatter on the other car's windshield. Worried that this was blood, guts, or other human parts, he jumped out of his car and rushed to see if he could help. When he opened their car door, he saw an elderly couple who looked at him with shocked expressions. An empty bowl sat on the woman's lap, which had recently held spaghetti and meatballs, which they were bringing to someone's house for dinner. The accident left Steven's car severely damaged. After the police arrived, they arranged for a tow truck to take Steven's car away. As if final exams, papers, and deploying to Iraq weren't enough, he now had to worry about getting his car repaired.

Our family visited Steven in January 2006, a few days before he headed to Camp Shelby, MS, for training. We tried to redirect Steven's attention from what he'd soon be facing by going out to dinner and relaxing together.

2

Call To Service

WHEN I VISITED STEVEN AT FT. BENNING, during his basic training, I began considering joining the military. Although I have always respected the military, I did not feel a deeply personal call to serve until September 11, 2001.

I took a career aptitude test in high school that pointed me toward becoming a corporate executive or an FBI agent. While taking it, I didn't think much of the test, but being an FBI agent sounded interesting. Upon investigation, I found out that Accounting was one of the top college majors for someone interested in joining the FBI. I liked the fact that it wasn't only sitting behind a desk and crunching numbers. There was also an element of action to it. If I studied accounting in college, I could please my parents by going to college and still have the action involved with law enforcement in a few years.

After graduating high school, I attended Bryant College in Smithfield, RI. I started making my way through the required classes that I needed to get my accounting degree. I was always somewhat of an early bird, and I tended to opt for courses earlier in the morning if I could help it.

September 11, 2001, was during my sophomore year of college. As I made my way to an early psychology class that morning, I overheard vague details about a plane crash. In my pre-caffeinated daze, I wrote it off as an accident and continued to class. There wasn't much I could do about it anyway. Our professor was late to class and told us she was watching the news about the plane crashes.

"Wait, crashes? As in plural? More than one?" I thought to myself. She had my attention. As some of the students had already heard, she announced that two planes crashed into the World Trade Center towers in New York. When the conversation escalated in the room, she figured there was little chance of teaching anything that day, so she dismissed us. I can only assume that she also wanted to get back to the television to see what was happening.

As I made my way back to my dorm, I purposely walked through a common area in a building where a TV was almost always on. As I watched, a CNN Breaking News report appeared on the screen: "Fire reported at Pentagon." I was sure at that moment that none of it happened by accident. But it sure looked like something out of a Hollywood movie. I spent the rest of the day watching the news reports in my room. Each new account that came in left me feeling more and more enraged at the attacks. It was sickening to see our nation's capital attacked, New York's iconic skyline collapse, and a tragedy in Pennsylvania.

When I learned of the crash in Pennsylvania, I thought of my father because he was in Pennsylvania. Since he traveled so often, I didn't keep track of each trip, but I knew he was in Pennsylvania this time. Fearing the absolute worst, I tried calling him on his cell phone. No luck. "Shit," I thought. I called my mother at home to see if she had been able to reach him, which she had. She told me that my father was consulting at a building not far from where United Airlines Flight 93 went down.

My father later told us about how the initial reports of the crash affected that community in Pennsylvania. A frantic group of parents raced out of the building where he was working. On the local radio station, the employees heard that a plane had crashed into a school. Fearful parents ran to get their children out of school in case theirs was the next one targeted. With nothing left for my father to do for work, he returned to his hotel to figure out how to get home. The United States began grounding all flights, so he couldn't fly home as he had intended. He awoke to find his hotel lobby swarming with FBI agents, FAA officials, and every other three-letter acronym under the sun. As my dad ate his continental breakfast, the agents set up a makeshift command center in the hotel's dining area. There were about 50 FBI agents in the room getting briefed on what had happened the day before. My dad sat through the entire briefing as they showed satellite photos and other information. He knew that he was witnessing a historical moment in that room, and much to his surprise, he wasn't asked to leave the area.

As there were no flights available, he decided to drive his rental car back home to Connecticut. Along the way, he met stranded business people who were hitching rides back home with truckers.

As I reflected on the events of that day, I thought that I would want to be a part of the military response to these attacks if that became necessary. I wondered if I should drop out of college and join the Army or finish out my next three years of school first.

Like with any big life decision I've ever made, I chose to sleep on it. News reports suggested that we were in this one for the long haul, unlike any prior military actions during my lifetime. Any military response would likely take place over several years. By the end of that semester, I had decided to graduate before joining the military. If there were still a need after I graduated, I'd join then. My parents had invested enough into my education that I felt like I owed them to see it through. And, in May of 2004, I earned my accounting degree right in the meaty part of the GPA bell curve. Instead of working for the FBI as I had envisioned, I worked for a regional accounting firm auditing and preparing taxes.

At this point, four years had passed since 9/11, and it was clear that the war's end wasn't coming anytime soon. I knew a little more about what it meant to join the Army from hearing Steven's stories. I believed that if he could handle it, so could I. After considering the idea of enlisting, I decided to give Steven a call to get his advice. His reaction was, "Holy shit! That's great! What do mom and dad think?" I replied, "You are the only one who knows about this right now, and I'd like to keep it that way until I've made up my mind for sure." He told me about the typical basic training day that involves a lot of exercise, drill sergeants screaming in your face, and very little sleep. I asked him to talk me out of it, to give me all the reasons in the world why I shouldn't join the Army. I knew it would be an exercise in futility, but I figured I should know all the bad stuff too.

After I spoke with Steven, I decided to sleep on the decision to enlist for a few days. It was the most significant decision I had to make in my life so far, and it would affect me for at least the next eight years of my life. Eight years was the minimum commitment a new soldier needed to make to the Army at that time. Six of those were in an active status, plus another two in the Inactive Ready Reserve (IRR), where you could get called back to duty. I needed to be sure I wouldn't immediately regret the decision.

The Army was not like other decisions I'd made, such as where I wanted to attend college or where I wanted to work. I couldn't back out of the Army if I didn't like it. I could have transferred to another college or found another job if either of those didn't work out. The Army isn't like that. If I changed my mind about this, I would have no easy way to get out of it since you're committed to serving the entire length of your contract. I later would find out there are some circumstances where you can get out of your contract early.

Then one day, I heard a news report that angered me. For 2005, the Army, and the National Guard, in particular, were not likely to hit their recruiting targets for the year. Where was that American pride we all felt after September 11th? It dawned on me that I was young and able-bodied, so why shouldn't I join the military? I was representative of everything that angered me, so if I couldn't step up and join, how could I expect anyone else to join?

Screw the fact that I had a college degree, a good job, and every reason in the world not to join the military. That kind of logic was what was eating me up in the first place—enough excuses and procrastination. I was going to do this, and nothing was going to stand in my way. That is except telling my parents. The drill sergeants screaming at me, getting shot at, or worse, did not bother me as much as my fear of telling my parents about this decision.

So one night, in late October 2005, my parents, Steven and Leeza, and I all went out for my mother's birthday dinner. "It can't wait any longer," I told myself. "Tonight has to be the night I tell them." With my brother's support, I managed to break the news to them in the middle of our dinner. Following that, I jokingly said, "Happy birthday, Mom!" to ease the tension. She responded to my joke with a half-smile and a worried look in her eyes. It wasn't that she didn't like my decision, but she was concerned with having both of her boys in the military during a time of war. After I ruined my mother's 49th birthday, Steven assured my parents that I could handle the things he had gone through. Steven drove Leeza and me while my parents went in their car when we headed home from that dinner. I can only imagine the conversation my parents had, if there was one at all. Ours was a quiet car ride, but I felt an immense sense of pride and excitement over sharing my decision. I was going to be a soldier, but there was still one thing I had to do. I needed to make it official.

The next day, I took a day off from work to visit the Connecticut Army National Guard Armory in Manchester, CT. I didn't want to waste any more time thinking about this. While I could have decided to enlist as an active-duty soldier, I chose the National Guard instead. Enlisting in the National Guard would allow me to remain at my civilian job, which I liked, and let me continue living in Connecticut. Once you complete Basic Training and AIT, a National Guard training differs from full-time active-duty soldiers. Guard soldiers only train one weekend each month and two full weeks per year, while active-duty soldiers train all year-round.

The recruiter I met with told me all the information I needed to put together to enlist. Early the next week, I returned with all the paperwork I needed. My recruiter then scheduled a time for me to go to the Military Entrance Processing Station (MEPS) at Westover Air Reserve Base. This MEPS location is where all recruits from New England begin their military careers. We took the Armed Services Vocational Aptitude Battery (ASVAB) testing, which is like the military's version of the SATs. We also had to endure physical and medical qualification tests as well as a background evaluation.

My time at MEPS took place over two days. The first day I arrived late in the day, so I could only finish the ASVAB test. Then I went to the "barracks" for the night. I've stayed at some hotels that weren't quite as nice as these barracks were. It turns out I was staying at The Flyers Inn, an Air Force lodging facility. After seeing the posh accommodations the Air Force had to offer, I suspected that I might have chosen the wrong branch of service! The room even included a menu for room service.

The following day, I reported bright and early to begin the medical screening. This screening consisted of a thorough physical exam. It included height, weight, hearing, and vision tests. It also included drug and alcohol testing, muscle and joint range of motion tests, among several others.

Once I passed the exams, I met with someone to review my contract. While I was aware of the commitment I was making, the counselor made sure that I knew the specifics of the contract I was entering. He also discussed the various job opportunities available to me. He told me that I was eligible for the Officer Candidate School (OCS) because I already had a four-year college degree. Since my ASVAB scores were very high, he said I could do well in a field like intelligence or linguistics.

This counselor could have said little to be able to change my mind. I informed him that I wished to enlist as an infantryman. He made several more attempts to change my mind, and every time my answer was still the same.

Some people have asked me why I enlisted instead of becoming an officer. Officers need a college degree, which I had, so it would have been as easy for me to start with a higher rank (and pay) as it would be to enlist at a much lower rank. Enlisted soldiers often do not have degrees when they enter the military. So, becoming an officer is not even an option for them without extra schooling. It was for me, yet I still decided to enlist.

The reason was pretty simple. I respected the hell out of my brother, and I was proud of him for serving. I never intended to make him feel like his service was less valuable or even outrank him. Throughout our time in the military, there was rarely a time where I outranked him. When I graduated basic training, we were both E-4 Specialists. We were both promoted to E-5 Sergeants within about a month of each other. I never wanted him to feel inferior to me.

While I could fulfill all the suggested roles, I knew my country needed infantrymen at that point since we were engaging in a ground war. As if to accept defeat, the MEPS counselor printed the paperwork where I would sign over the next eight years of my life to the Army. I then headed to the room where recruits get sworn in. On November 9, 2005, I raised my right hand and repeated after the naval officer who swore me in:

I, Scott DeLuzio, do solemnly swear that I will support and defend the Constitution of the United States and the State of Connecticut against all enemies, foreign and domestic; that I will bear true faith and allegiance to the same; and that I will obey the orders of the President of the United States and the Governor of Connecticut and the orders of the officers appointed over me, according to law and regulations. So help me, God.

Shortly after swearing–in, I met with another counselor who would schedule me to go to basic training. Since I was still working at the accounting firm at the time, I wanted to make sure that my employer would have plenty of notice of my extended leave. I didn't want them to have to reschedule my work because I decided to join the Army. The counselor told me that I could schedule my report date for basic training any time up to one year out. I knew that I couldn't wait a whole year, so I decided on early March 2006. My orders read:

"With consent of the Governor of CONNECTICUT, you are ordered to initial active duty for training (IADT)... Report to: 30th Adjutant General Battalion (Reception), Ft Benning, GA Reporting date: 07 March 2006"

The next thing I had to do was tell my employer that I was going away for about three and a half months for basic training. From then on, they also needed to know that I could get called to active duty for any state or federal emergency or deployed overseas. I was no longer another employee. From here on out, I was also a soldier. The following week, I drafted a letter to the company's HR department stating my intentions. She told me that she respected my decision and would communicate it to the rest of the company. I was relieved that she took the news so well because I wanted to keep my job. At the time, I wasn't aware of the employment protection laws that would have prohibited me from getting fired for joining the National Guard. So, I was pretty nervous going into that meeting.

With that behind me, I had to start working on my plan to be in great shape by March. Every morning before work, I would run a few miles and lift weights. I started paying attention to what I ate for the first time and tried losing weight by cutting out junk food. As I learned from Steven's experience in basic training, I also knew I would have to kick my pretty serious coffee habit. I couldn't go cold turkey from having survived on it throughout much of high school and college. I had thrived on it while working late hours at the accounting firm. I weaned myself off of coffee instead of undergoing painful withdrawals and suffering at basic training.

On March 6, 2006, my mother drove me to the Army National Guard armory in Enfield, CT, to meet my recruiter. He would bring me back up to the MEPS station at Westover Air Reserve Base to begin my path through basic training. When my mother left me there, I gave her a hug and a kiss goodbye as she tried to choke back tears. With Steven deployed to Iraq, for the first time, both of her sons would be away with the Army at the same time.

My recruiter was finishing up some paperwork when I arrived, so I had to wait for about 15 minutes before leaving. Those 15 minutes seemed like an eternity. I wanted to get it over with—like the painful anticipation before tearing off a Band-Aid. We made small talk during the 25-minute drive to MEPS, but I kept thinking there was no turning back now. I was on my way to basic training.

When we arrived at MEPS, I got placed in a group of recruits, with most going into active duty. Regardless of which branch we were embarking on, we had to fill out more paperwork. I must have filled out a stack of forms an inch thick that day. When we were finally done late at night, we got sent to the same nice "barracks" that I was in a few months before. In contrast to the almost giddy feeling I had when I joined the Army, I found it hard to sleep. Alone in that room, the gravity of what I was doing started to sink in.

I had to be up early again to rejoin my group and receive our flight information. Everyone was going to different places in the country, so very few of us got on the same flight. Most of us flew out of Bradley International Airport in Connecticut, only a short drive away from the MEPS facility. We boarded a blue school bus to get us there. While I tried to keep to myself, I was slightly amused to overhear some of the conversations. Future Air Force cooks argued that their jobs would be much more challenging than the future Army MPs. To which, the prospective MPs argued back. It reminded me of the mid-90's Pauly Shore movie *In the Army Now*: "We're the few, the proud, The WATERBOYS!" In the film, Pauly Shore's character had no idea what he was getting into either. It was funny because I realized none of them knew how hard their job would be. I didn't either, but I knew they all couldn't be right.

I was sitting next to a younger woman who was fidgeting and talking almost non-stop. She was nervous about joining the military, and I hoped to escape her nervous energy when we got to the airport. I didn't need her ramblings ramping up my nerves any more than they already were.

I knew my home airport well and made a quick dash for the security checkpoint. We received our boarding passes back at MEPS and didn't need to check any luggage. My recruiter and Steven told me I wouldn't get to use any of the "civilian" items I brought with me, so I didn't pack much. After getting through security, I bought some lunch. As I was making my way to a table, the woman from the bus spotted me and asked to sit with me. I lied and told her that I had to get to my gate because my flight was leaving soon. As I headed away from her, I worried that she'd be on the same flight, or worse, she'd have a seat next to me, but luckily, I didn't see her again. Later, I felt like a jerk for blowing her off. At the time, her nervous rambling was making me more anxious, and I needed to get away from the situation.

When I got up to board the plane, I recall thinking, "This is it. There's no turning back now." I had taken this same flight to Atlanta before, but this one seemed to go much faster because I managed to fall asleep, which I rarely do on airplanes. I was grateful for that because Steven had told me never to take sleep for granted in basic training.

Recruits arrived in Atlanta from all over the country. After getting off our plane, we waited in an area that resembled a cattle holding pen for our transportation to Ft. Benning. When our bus finally arrived, we got herded onto it. With no one accompanying us other than the bus driver, we had two more hours to be alone. I took the opportunity to sleep again, which made the ride seem like 15 minutes. Because I had been to Ft. Benning before to visit Steven, I knew we were very close when I noticed a giant cow statue in front of a Best Buy off the highway. When we pulled in at 0015 (15 minutes past midnight), the knot in my stomach was now enormous. Despite everything Steven had told me to prepare, I was more nervous than at any other time in my entire life.

A drill sergeant waited at the curb for us as we approached the 30th Adjutant General building. The bus doors opened, and he stepped aboard. I don't remember what he said verbatim, but it was something along these lines:

"HEY, LISTEN UP! I will be your drill sergeant while at reception until you get assigned to your training company. You have chosen to join the Army during a time of war. The other drill sergeants and I respect your decision to do so. Do not confuse this respect with us being soft on you. You will only make things worse for yourself if you do. NOW GET OFF MY BUS! MOVE, MOVE, MOVE!"

I swear city buses should have drill sergeants for bus drivers. They will triple the speed people get on and off their buses.

We then rushed into an initial reception room to begin our in-processing. Here, the drill sergeants barked more orders at us in what I would call "typical drill sergeant voice." The drill sergeant said that the quicker we got everything done, the more sleep we would get that night.

We had about two hours of processing to get through before letting us go to our new barracks. The first stop was to collect more paperwork to confirm we were in the right place. Next, we all took a turn visiting an "amnesty room."

The amnesty room is where you get a free pass to turn in any contraband you might have brought with you. Whether you knew you brought contraband or not, everyone went inside. Each amnesty room had a bench and a hole in the wall, a little larger than a mail slot. The hole in the wall was where the drill sergeants told us to deposit any contraband. A list of prohibited items was hanging on the wall above the mail slot. Food, playing cards, cell phones, pornography, weapons, drugs, alcohol, and tobacco were prohibited.

Many people have at least one of these items with them when they first enter. An innocent soda from the airport or a pack of gum they bought for the plane ride can find its way into this room. There's nothing wrong with having it when you arrive, but it needs to get disposed of in the amnesty room. One drill sergeant told us about a kid from Texas who had his grandfather's revolver that he always carried with him. In the box, it went, gone forever. No one gets back the things they drop in the amnesty box.

We got about 60 seconds in the amnesty room before the drill sergeants told us to get out. I learned that everything we would do from here on out would get done very fast.

The drill sergeant finally showed us to the barracks and told us we'd be waking up at 0345. We had to shower and get whatever other personal hygiene we needed out of the way before sleeping. At this point, it was after 0200 in the morning, meaning we'd have less than two hours of sleep that night. I soon realized why Steven had been so tired when we visited him about a year and a half earlier.

Day One

The following day we got our Physical Training (PT) uniforms, received briefs on various topics, and got our vaccinations. I had seven vaccinations, most of which I'd never heard of before. Since I'm allergic to penicillin, I avoided getting that shot in my ass like everyone else. Those who ended up getting it had an uncomfortable time sitting and walking over the next 24-48 hours. In the Post Exchange (PX), all thirty of us had five minutes to buy any essentials we didn't already have. To see how impossible of a task this was, the next time you go to a drug store, try timing it. It will likely take you at least 10 minutes to find a few things, especially if you haven't been to that particular store before.

Next, we had the least personable shopping experience ever. The folks who issued our PT uniforms were the opposite of the friendly, helpful salespeople you'd see at a clothing store. We entered a warehouse-style room with lines painted on the concrete floors, so we did not veer off course (more of that "cattle" feel). Waiting by the door was a civilian employee, who sized us up and down and pointed to the station where we should go. "Fatties to the left, skinnies to the right, and everyone else in the middle." The civilian pointed me towards the middle to catch my PT uniform as it got tossed to me.

Day Two

My impression that everything had to get done fast when I first arrived at Ft. Benning proved correct. I couldn't figure out why though, since we also had plenty of downtime. In a way, this was my introduction to the phrase "hurry up and wait." Uncle Sam wasn't paying me to think at this point, though, so I went along for the ride. The second day was not as busy and only consisted of a vision test and issuing our Army Combat Uniforms (ACUs). The slower day was a relief for most people in my group who had gotten pretty ill from all the shots they received the day before. I don't think they could have handled much more that day.

Most of the week-and-a-half we spent at reception was pretty dull. We received new pieces of our uniforms sporadically like they forgot to give them to us the first time. There were more briefings, and we got our new haircuts, which were all shaved to nearly bald. We also received our dog tags, which only is memorable because I couldn't get the chain clasp to work on mine. The person who issued the dog tags got in a few "Gomer Pyle" jokes at my expense while I was struggling. Then he took the dog tags to try connecting them himself. He couldn't make it work either because one of the ends had become bent. After he accepted defeat, he got me a new chain.

On Friday, March 17, 2006, we were assigned to our basic training companies. We lined up in formation and got introduced to the drill sergeants whose job it was to turn us into soldiers over the next few months. One drill sergeant noticed I was wearing the Specialist (E-4) enlisted rank instead of starting as a Private (E-1) like most others. Poking my chest where the rank was, he asked, "Why the hell are you wearing that?" What he was trying to ask was, "How did a recruit get to be a Specialist and skip being a Private?" I avoided drawing any further attention to myself by answering the question I knew he was asking. I replied, "because I went to college, drill sergeant!" I couldn't think of anything else to say at that moment, and that was the truth. Upon letting out a suspicious, "HA!" he got an inch from my face and asked, "You want to die, don't you?" Before I could respond, he moved on to harass the next Private.

The drill sergeants then herded us onto a cattle car, which took us to our new barracks. I'm no longer loosely comparing us to cattle to make a point. Fifty of us plus our duffle bags full of equipment stood on a truck with bars on the windows and benches on the side. We were not allowed to use the benches as seats. Instead, the drill sergeants told us to stand on them. I thought I would gain a little extra space by standing on the bench for the entire ride since I could hover over the people standing on the floor a bit. I was wrong, and at 6'1" tall, I had to hunch over the whole time to avoid hitting my head on the roof. Even that didn't work very well as we went over bumpy railroad tracks at least a half-dozen times.

After finishing basic training, I looked at a map and found only one set of railroad tracks between the reception building to our new barracks. It was apparent then that they were driving back and forth, trying to make the ride as miserable as possible. They succeeded.

The first week at basic training consisted of issuing our TA-50 field equipment. TA-50 refers to the Table of Allowances 50, which lists all the equipment issued to each soldier based on their military occupation and location. The equipment given to us consisted of canteens, ponchos, rucksacks, and entrenching tools (E-Tool/shovel). Our M-16 rifles and our Kevlar vests and helmets were issued to us as well during that first week. The drill sergeants showed us how to make our bunks and place our belongings in our wall lockers. We had to do these things precisely to teach us to have attention to detail. This week also included "getting smoked" a lot.

Getting smoked refers to the corrective exercises we did. Things like push-ups, flutter kicks, crab walks, and others with funny names like "Jo-Jo the Duck". Jo-Jo the Duck is where you assume a baseball catcher's position, place your hands on your head, and walk like a duck. You then have to repeat the phrase *"I'm Jo-Jo the Duck, and I'm all fucked up."* We would have to do these exercises whenever someone or the whole group messed up or failed a task.

Sometimes the smoke sessions were not distributed fairly. In those cases, the drill sergeants stopped smoking that recruit and smoked all the others before him while he watched and stood at attention. The idea is that one of two things will happen. (1) The screw-up will feel guilty about their buddies getting smoked and work harder not to mess up, or (2) the rest of the group will "correct" them with hog-tied cold showers or other punishments. Guilting the recruits into correcting themselves is the more desirable outcome.

One task given to us early on was to fill our canteens up to the very top, so the water did not make a sloshing noise when the drill sergeants shook it. Then we had to chug the entire canteen. If one person didn't fill their canteen all the way, we would have to do the whole thing again after getting smoked for their failure.

On top of exercises for failing to complete pointless tasks, we got punished whenever someone let it slip that it was their birthday.

My birthday took place in March, a few days after getting to Ft. Benning. My birthday was one of the first of the fifty or so guys in our training platoon. I managed to keep mine a secret from everyone, including the drill sergeants. I knew from Steven's experience that birthdays are not a pleasant experience. A few days later, another private let it slip that his birthday had passed. After returning from lunch at the chow hall, we saw how drill sergeants celebrate birthdays for the first time. They dismantled every single bunk with poles of different lengths scattered around the barracks. They crammed all the mattresses into the latrine so tight that you couldn't walk inside it without removing some of them. Anyone who forgot to put a lock on their wall locker had their belongings thrown into an enormous pile. The drill sergeants told us we had an hour to put all the bunks back together and sort all the crap that got scattered throughout the room from the unlocked lockers. With roughly 60 beds in the barracks, there were 30 bunks, giving us at most two minutes to put each bunk back together. It was an impossible task, so we got smoked again for failing to meet the time standard.

Holidays (or quasi-holidays at least) brought similar shenanigans. On April Fool's day, the drill sergeants woke us up screaming that someone had vandalized a stairwell. They told us the vandals had written something not-so-nice about one of the drill sergeants. I won't put in writing what it was. Let's just say something homosexual in nature. They used this as an excuse to smoke us all day long until someone fessed up to the vandalism. Of course, no one did it, so no one confessed. Some of the recruits even started turning on one another, saying, "I saw that Private do it." Fistfights even broke out over the accusations. The next day, the drill sergeants dropped the subject altogether. When someone brought it up a few weeks later, the drill sergeants even pretended like they didn't know about the incident. I'm all for a good April Fool's joke, and they got us pretty good with that one.

Dispersed through all the seemingly pointless "hazing" going on was some actual training. We learned how to use the various weapons in the US Army Infantry's arsenal. The weapons included the bigger guns like the M-2 or "Ma Deuce," the shoulder-fired AT-4, the M-249 Squad Automatic Weapon (SAW), and the M-240B machine gun. It also included the M-203 grenade launcher, the M-67 fragmentation grenade, bayonet, and, of course, our M-16 rifles.

There was also hands-on training, such as first-aid tactics. We trained with scenarios like getting an injured soldier out of hostile areas using different carry techniques. One of the training exercises involved clearing an airway if someone was choking or having difficulty breathing. It seemed like an unlikely scenario in combat, but it is generally good to know, so I paid close attention. I was fortunate to have remembered this training years later when my son started choking on an apple slice. When I recognized he was choking, the training kicked in, and I cleared it out a few seconds later. The training also reinforced the need to stay calm in stressful scenarios, which allows you to focus on what needs to get done without panicking.

There was plenty of other training that I am hoping not ever to need in real life. For example, the gas chamber seemed to be one of the drill sergeant's favorite training days. They issued us pro-masks (gas masks) the night before, and a drill sergeant checked each of our masks to ensure it had a proper fit. I suspected that mine didn't fit, but the drill sergeant cocked his head to the side and said, "Yea, you'll be alright," then tossed my mask back to me. I didn't question him. After all, what did I know about these masks? The following day, we were all told to have a full cup of milk at breakfast. We were then herded into the gas chamber wearing our masks. The doors closed, and the CS gas got released. CS gas is also known as tear gas.

After most of us gained confidence that we could breathe with our masks even as the gas surrounded us, the drill sergeants tested us. They told us to remove the masks, say our name and the last four digits of our Social Security number, put the mask back on, and clear the gas out of it. Because my mask didn't have a great seal to begin with, I was coughing and had tears filling my eyes almost from the moment we entered the chamber. When I went to say my name and SSN, I had a string of snot and stringy saliva running down to my waist. The milk the drill sergeants had us drink earlier increased the stringiness of the snot and saliva. It sucked, yet the drill sergeants were waiting for us with video cameras laughing as we were tripping over our feet to get out of there. I would bet that you can find it on YouTube if you look hard enough.

Another gem of a training event was the rappel tower. It's three stories high, and I have always been afraid of heights. Being up on a ladder, walking near a cliff's edge, or being too close to the railing on the mall's second floor always bothered me. As I scaled the cargo net ladder to the top of the tower, the drill sergeant could tell how scared I was. It felt like I got clipped onto an itty-bitty rope and carabiner that could never support my weight. I don't know if it was my hands or legs shaking that gave it away. He screamed at me to move faster, so I hopped over the wall. As I got ready to start my descent, the drill sergeant looked over and said, "Holy shit, your ropes are coming undone! Give me your hand!"

I may have achieved flight that day as I scrambled back up the wall. When I got back to the top of the wall, he started hysterically laughing at me and assured me that I was okay. "Dick," I thought to myself. I did make it down on my own and started questioning what I was getting into joining the Army.

Meals during basic training get eaten very fast. We usually had only a few minutes to get the entire platoon of over 50 guys through the chow hall. If you got caught talking or doing anything the drill sergeants didn't like, they told you to throw out whatever food you hadn't finished. It didn't matter if you hadn't even taken a bite yet.

We were fortunate to have MREs (Meals Ready to Eat) when we were in the field. MREs contain a whole 1200-calorie meal in a durable bag. They include an entrée, side dish, crackers or bread, peanut butter, cheese spread, a flameless heater bag to heat your food, and a dessert or candy item. The candies always had to get turned over to the drill sergeants after opening our meals. They would then taunt us by eating the candy in front of us. I considered eating MREs "fortunate" because we usually had more time to eat out in the field, plus it seemed like we'd get more food than we got in the chow hall. During basic training, I was always so hungry that I would eat my MRE cold to get in as much as possible in the short amount of time allotted to us.

We had our share of troublemakers while at basic training. For one reason or another, a handful of people decided to go Absent Without Leave (AWOL). One of these people had received a diagnosis a few days earlier of liver disease. He was going to receive an honorable medical discharge shortly after his diagnosis. He most likely would have received a disability check for the rest of his life, courtesy of Uncle Sam.

Going AWOL put a stop to that. He later received a dishonorable discharge with no benefits. He may even have a tough time finding a job of any type now, never mind one with a good health insurance plan.

When Basic Training was over, I was so eager to take a 36-hour break before AIT started as Steven had. As they had done for Steven, my parents were flying down to meet me, and I was psyched. It had been 82 days since my mother dropped me off at the National Guard Armory, and I was looking forward to a break. Our drill sergeants told us that we were not to see family during this time. I don't know if they were messing with us or not, but I told my parents to meet me down the road from our barracks since they had already booked their flight. Luckily, they got a rental car with tinted back windows, making it easier for my "stealth" getaway. Maybe the drill sergeants were messing with us by saying this, but I didn't want to find out. With my parents, it was so nice to eat food at a more human pace. At the hotel, I used a computer to check my email and see if I could chat with anyone from home. I connected with Steven's girlfriend, Leeza. She let it slip that Steven was going to be home from Iraq for my graduation. That news was supposed to be a surprise. I was happy, though, that there was an end in sight for him. I even got to talk

27

to Steven for a few minutes when he called my dad. It was good to be able to compare notes about basic training. Those 36 hours went by way too fast.

After my parents dropped me off, I joined the guys standing around talking about what they did on their pass. We weren't supposed to be talking, though, and we ended up having to do some push-ups. It was amazing how fast we could go from well-disciplined soldiers to a disorganized gaggle in under 36 hours.

The next day after our pass was Memorial Day. Time had flown by so fast that I didn't have a chance to notice that it was already the end of May. We had a lot of downtime because it was a holiday, which pissed me off. I figured that we could have finished basic training two weeks sooner if we used holidays and some Sundays as training days instead of "down" days. It was hard to be in a bad mood, though. Between the conversation with Steven I had over the weekend and realizing that I only had a month before I would be out of there, I was in a pretty good mood.

Before we graduated, we had to get through a week-long Field Training Exercise (FTX), a 12-mile road march, and a recovery week. To test our skills, the FTX incorporated many things we learned over the last few months. We had some realistic scenarios based on actual situations a unit could face in combat. At the end of the FTX, we returned to our barracks by doing a 12-mile road march. I found it funny that they labeled this as a "road march" because most of it was not on the road at all. Much of it was walking through the woods and a river in knee-deep water with all our equipment. I thought that would suck, but I was already wet from sweat, so it felt nice to cool off in the water.

We had missions to accomplish along the way, like taking out an enemy sniper position in the woods. As my team made our way around to where we thought the sniper was, we encountered our Commanding Officer (CO) acting as a civilian with information for us. Since he was in the sniper's area, we couldn't tell if he was a friendly civilian or an enemy sniper. Each time we asked him to stop and get on the ground, he would run away.

One of the other guys and I ended up chasing him down with our weapons fixed on him. I got close enough that I was able to grab his collar and throw him to the ground. Throwing him to the ground was a rather bold move on my part. At any other time, the very act of touching a superior during basic training would have been enough to get the whole platoon smoked for hours. But, as I approached him, I hesitated as if to say, "OK, I caught him. Now what?" Sensing my reluctance to restrain him, CO whispered, "It's alright. It's all part of the game."

I thought, "Game on, sir!" After throwing him to the ground, I followed up with a knee in his back and began searching him for intelligence. He gave me some information about a chest with "golden treasure" located nearby.

A treasure chest? Was this for real? I thought this was basic training, not some pirate movie. Anyhow, we had him lead us to where this "treasure" was, which turned out to be a heavy wooden crate. We managed to open it and found the "golden treasure" to be our Infantry Crossed Rifles Pin. It was the first time many of us had seen the crossed rifles, and it gave us a sudden surge of energy and excitement. The wave of excitement was a good thing because we had to carry the crate with us for the rest of the 12-mile march.

The road march ended at a place called "Honor Hill." Here we all stood at attention around a bonfire and listened to the First Sergeant give a speech. We were each handed our canteen cups filled with "grog," a combination of Gatorade, water, and dry ice. Many people think there is alcohol in the grog - there isn't. While standing in formation, the drill sergeants came around to each of us and pinned our cross rifles. They asked everyone, "Do you want it pinned like a man or like a bitch?" They were trying to ask whether you want it pinned to your shirt the way they're supposed to be (like a bitch) or pinned into your chest (like a man). If I recall correctly, pretty much everyone chose to have them pinned on "like a man."

While standing in formation, I started to get a little lightheaded. Sometimes, while standing up, you will "lock" your knees straight. If you do this long enough, you will pass out. The problem is not that your knees are locked, but rather the muscles in your legs are not getting used. Your heart relies on the muscle contractions in your legs to push the blood through your legs. When your knees lock, the knee joint provides you with balance, not your leg muscles. Since this causes the blood to stop flowing, the blood flow to your brain drops, and shortly after, you'll drift off to dreamland for a little while. A little flex in your knee is all it takes to get the blood flowing again, which occurs once you collapse to the ground.

As I started feeling lightheaded, I realized that I had locked my knees. I tried bending my knees a bit to get the blood flowing again, but it was already too late. I turned to the guy to my right and said, "Hey, I'm going down." Unfortunately for me, he was now a well-disciplined soldier. He didn't move a muscle, and I fell flat on my face. The next thing I remember was sitting on the ground behind formation with three other guys from my platoon who also passed out right after me. One of the drill sergeants came over and joked, "What's the problem? You made it through the FTX but fell out of the formation!"

Other than the shenanigans on the rappel tower and April Fool's Day, this was pretty much the first time the drill sergeant joked with us. I was pretty sure I was dreaming at this point. It turns out that I wasn't. After pinning us with our cross rifles, the drill sergeants started treating us like humans. We were allowed a few luxuries, such as using all the utensils in the chow hall, not just the spoon. We even got to listen to the radio. Most people who went through basic training will tell you that they never could listen to the radio. We only got one chance to listen to the radio, which was in our last week right before graduation. It was the first music we heard outside of the horrible singing in the showers in months. I found that sometimes little things go a long way to boost morale.

Finally, on June 22, 2006, my parents, brother, and my Uncle Bob arrived in Georgia for my Turning Blue ceremony. I was on cloud nine. A Turning Blue ceremony is where new infantrymen get presented with their "blue cords." The blue cord is what distinguishes infantrymen from other soldiers in their dress uniforms. The infantry blue cord is a US Army decoration worn over the right shoulder of all qualified US Army infantrymen. It served as a morale booster for the infantrymen fighting in the Korean War. It continues to be worn on the dress uniforms of all US Army infantrymen today. Steven, who recently returned from Iraq, would present me with mine, as I had done for him.

That morning, we had an inspection by our Sergeant Major. It was one of those inspections where no matter how clean or squared away something is, he would find something wrong. Even if it weren't, he'd say it was wrong to make you do some push-ups. It didn't matter. My family was downstairs waiting for me, and a million push-ups couldn't have brought me down.

We went down to the company area where the Turning Blue ceremony would take place. Our families were already down there and sitting in bleachers surrounding us. The ceremony itself was short. The CO and First Sergeant took turns explaining the skills we had learned and what it meant to become an infantryman. It was a chilling reminder that while we should be proud of our accomplishments, the realities of a nation at war still exist. They also reminded us that we would likely have to use the skills we learned in Iraq or Afghanistan soon.

When the time came, Steven put the cord on me. It meant a lot to me that Steven could be there to present me with my blue cord. I had looked up to him since he joined the military and was proud of his service in Iraq. It was an honor for me to present him with his cord. Still, it was even more of an honor to have a recently returned combat infantryman present me with my cord.

The next day, June 23, 2006, was graduation day. If I wasn't excited already, I was now! Like Steven had the summer before, we had another brief ceremony on the parade field across the street from our company area. The day was a typical, hot Georgia summer day, so most family members were dripping in sweat when the ceremony was over. As soon as we got released, I grabbed my things and took off to my parent's rental car as fast as possible. We made the two-hour drive back to Atlanta, joking and catching up the whole way.

Steven didn't talk much about his time in Iraq. It didn't seem like something he wanted to discuss anyway, so I didn't press the issue. I knew Steven had been through hell from the letter he sent me while I was in basic training. He'd get around to talking about it when the time was right. Instead, we discussed our plans to move in together and everything else we missed out on over the last few months. It was nice to finally head back home.

After Steven got home, he read the book *The Sheriff of Ramadi* by former Navy Seal Dick Couch. The book was mainly about the Navy Seals' actions during the Battle of Ramadi. However, Steven wrote a companion to the book he called *My Side*. In *My Side*, Steven writes:

> *I had very mixed feelings about reading this book and even more mixed feelings about writing these following pages. I feel like I haven't been able to speak about many of the things I did over there that were good because it reminds me too much of the bad. I wanted everyone to know what we did and why I'm proud of it, and this was the easiest way I could think of.*

My Side contains some pretty graphic descriptions and photos of their trucks after being hit by IEDs. When it got hit, Steven was the driver of one of these trucks. There was another photo of the destruction caused to a truck that killed a Lieutenant riding in it.

After reading both *The Sheriff of Ramadi* and *My Side*, it became clear that Steven had a lot to process when he got home.

Shortly after Steven returned from Iraq, he spoke to my parents about his college education. What he had experienced in Iraq was traumatic and made him appreciate his family and friends at home that much more. Steven didn't want to go back to Norwich, where he would be far away from pretty much everything and everyone important to him. Steven's feelings about being close to home persisted even years later while he was in Afghanistan. He posted on Facebook from Afghanistan in June 2010:

> *Funny, you spend so much time in your younger years making plans of escaping where you grew up, but the older you get, and the more time you spend around the world, the more you appreciate and miss home. Almost July, only a few more months...*

While Steven's grades weren't stellar, especially in the semester before leaving for Iraq, my dad helped him get accepted into his alma mater, the University of Hartford. Steven finished out his college education there, where he graduated cum laude.

3

Family and Country

A CO-WORKER OF MINE SET ME UP with a friend of hers, Vicki. We started dating in December of 2006, about six months after I finished basic training. We got married about a year and a half later, on August 30, 2008.

I didn't know much about Vicki when I first met her other than a few things my coworker told me about her. I wasn't seeing anyone at the time, and from what I knew, she seemed nice enough, so I figured we should meet up for a date. I made arrangements to meet her at a restaurant in her hometown, which was an area I wasn't familiar with at all. I had asked a friend of mine, who grew up in the same town as Vicki, to recommend a good restaurant in that area. Unfortunately, our date was on a Monday night, and the restaurant wasn't open on Mondays. When we arrived in the parking lot of the restaurant, all the lights were off. It was pitch black in the parking lot, and I looked like an ass because I had made it seem like I knew all about the place. Vicki suggested another restaurant a few miles away that would be open. We had a great time getting to know each other.

Vicki knew the restaurant I recommended wasn't open on Mondays. Still, she didn't want to embarrass me on the phone when I suggested it. Even though I worked long hours as an accountant during tax season, we continued to see each other as much as possible. Plus, being a soldier who was away for one weekend a month made it harder to carve out time for each other than it is for most couples.

About a year after we met, and because I've always been a bit of a geek, I proposed using a quiz I made with a Microsoft Excel spreadsheet. Each time she correctly answered questions about things we had done in our relationship, a part of an image would get revealed. After she answered the final question, "Will You Marry Me?" flashed over the screen. She knew I was a computer geek, so it was fitting that I'd put something together like this.

She sped through the quiz so fast that she had a few typos, and the way I programmed it, the "Will You Marry Me?" text was looking for exact responses. I had to tell her to go back and fix the typos so the proposal would work. I'm such a romantic.

The following months were busy with my long hours at work, wedding preparations, and Army training. A month before our wedding, I had my annual two-week training at Ft. Dix in New Jersey. It wasn't the best time to be away. Still, my soon-to-be wife learned that the Army doesn't always consider your personal life's schedule.

Shortly after our wedding, our unit was put on orders to deploy to Afghanistan sometime within the following year. With more than a year's notice, we had plenty of time to ensure that we took care of everything we needed to get squared away. There was a lot of training, weapons qualifications, and issuing new equipment to ensure we were ready for combat. We also had an extra three weeks of training during this pre-deployment cycle on top of our regular two weeks a year and one weekend a month training.

My family and I tried to keep on living our lives, keeping busy to not focus on the looming dangers of my upcoming deployment. Vicki and I didn't want to wait another year for me to return from Afghanistan to start a family. So, it thrilled us to announce to our families, in early 2009, that we were expecting our first child. They were overjoyed and stepped right up to support us in any way they could. They threw us baby showers, helped set up the nursery, and even drove Vicki to doctor's appointments. The pregnancy was a welcome distraction to the upcoming deployment.

Vicki was sick with H1N1, also known as "Swine Flu," near the end of her pregnancy. Vicki was admitted to the hospital with H1N1 right after I returned from the three-week training. I was also due to be away again in about two weeks. Since the virus was contagious and Vicki was in isolation, I only could visit her with a mask and gown. I felt like the doctors knew something I didn't know, though. They would enter her room wearing contraptions that looked like space suits with hoods and special breathing tubes. Meanwhile, I'd joke with Vicki that all they gave me was little more than a garbage bag and a tissue to hold over my face.

It was a scary time, though. Vicki was in the hospital for four days between the ICU and the maternity department so the doctors could observe our baby for fetal stress. Our unborn baby turned out fine, and after making a full recovery, Vicki got sent home to wait out the rest of the pregnancy.

We didn't know it at the time, but the CDC reported 280 pregnant women were admitted to the ICU with H1N1 (including my wife) during 2009. Out of those 280 women, 56 (20%) died from complications due to their illness. So, it was more severe than either of us realized at the time.

Soon after this ordeal, on November 21, 2009, our unit left for Camp Atterbury in Indiana. There we conducted more training, completed medical evaluations, and any paperwork that we needed to complete.

I was at Camp Atterbury for about a week when Vicki attempted to send me a Red Cross message that she had gone into labor.

Red Cross messages get verified before they go to a service member's command to inform them of an emergency. Because there wasn't yet a birth certificate, the Red Cross couldn't confirm that the birth was legitimate and wouldn't send a message. Instead, I informed my chain of command that my wife was in the hospital and would give birth within a few hours. My chain of command bent the rules a little to grant me emergency leave and book me on the next flight to Connecticut.

I had left for Indiana knowing I may miss my son's birth. I agonized over missing a call since the cell phone reception was spotty in the barracks and virtually non-existent in the field. Still, I was checking in with Vicki as often as I could. As soon as I found out that she was going into labor, I was determined to make it to the hospital in time. At that point, I had no time to spare since the airport was an hour away, and the flight was leaving in under two hours.

As soon as I reached the ticket counter, I explained my situation and asked if they could hold the flight. The ticket agent said he would do his best but that I needed to hurry. I had hoped my uniform would allow me to catch a break going through security. But the TSA agent made me go through the same screening as everyone else. I had to remove my boots, belt, dog tags, and everything else with metal as if I were any other traveler. I guess the TSA's thoroughness is good for security, but it didn't make me feel any better about making that flight. Upon making it through security, I began to sprint to get to my gate. I may have even knocked over a small child on the way to the gate. I was going to be a *great* dad!

I paid for the Wi-Fi on the flight to check my email to see if the baby decided to arrive early. My cell phone had broken while at Camp Atterbury, so I could only receive calls on it. I couldn't make calls or text. I had a very short layover in Atlanta, and as luck would have it, my connecting gate was next to a cell phone store. I had a few minutes to buy a new phone to replace my broken phone, so I pointed to one and said to the salesman, "I want that one." He tried to upgrade me and was a bit taken aback by my unwillingness to listen to his pitch. He called it "the quickest sale he ever made," though. If you've ever purchased a cell phone, you know that you never get out of there in 10 minutes, including transferring your phone number. It's incredible what a uniform and a no BS attitude can do for you! Once I got back in the air, I realized that the Wi-Fi plan I purchased on the last flight was good for 24 hours so that I could hop back on. No news came while I was in the air, but I was able to give my parents an update on my estimated arrival time so they would be able to pick me up when I landed.

I got in a little before midnight, and we drove for almost an hour to the hospital. At times my dad reached 100 MPH on the nearly empty highways in an attempt to make sure I got to the hospital in time. By the time I arrived, Vicki had already gotten a hefty dose of what she had referred to as the "good drugs" and felt the effects. The nurses checked her progress and indicated that we should get comfortable since it could still be a little while before the baby came. Only about thirty minutes went by when another nurse gasped, "There's his head!" On November 29, 2009, at 2:54 AM, we welcomed a healthy, 7 pound 11-ounce baby boy to the world. I had made it to the hospital with only about an hour to spare.

It was such a great feeling to be there for my son's birth, and I got ten days of leave that started the next day. I was able to experience all the new parent firsts like late-night feedings, changing dirty diapers, spit-up, and managing to get by on a few hours of sleep. These joys were overshadowed by knowing that I had to return to be with my unit in Indiana in a few days. Although, I do remember joking with some of my guys when I got back to Indiana when they asked if I missed being at home. I told them, "Hell, I get more sleep here!"

When I got back to Indiana, I got caught up on any briefings and vaccinations I had missed. We also did a lot of training in what's referred to as Military Operations in Urban Terrain (MOUT). MOUT consists of breaching and clearing buildings while moving together as a team. I have one exercise burned in my memory. It was a live-fire exercise, which uses real bullets instead of blanks. We were moving up a field towards a building while providing supporting fire to other soldiers moving in the same direction. This type of training wasn't new to us, but the ground was very wet, and each step had us sinking to our knees in the mud. We were also twisting our bodies to free our feet from the ground's muddy embrace as we were firing and falling - a lot. At one point, I stopped firing because I fell face-first into the mud, which caused the barrel of my rifle to go deep into the wet ground. If you've ever seen a Bugs Bunny and Elmer Fudd cartoon, you'll know that sticking something down the barrel of a gun and shooting it is a bad idea. That night I ended up cleaning my rifle in the shower to get all the mud out. It was a mess.

Our unit had arrived at Camp Atterbury a few weeks before Steven's unit did, but there was a time where we were both there. We got a chance to meet up on a couple of occasions when we both happened to have a few minutes of downtime. It was never for any more than five or 10 minutes. But, it was nice to catch up and see how each other was doing. It also allowed us to forget for a brief time that we'd be in a war zone in a few weeks.

Both Steven's unit and my unit received leave to return home for a few days around Christmas. Our units were bussing us back home - his unit to Vermont, where they were based, and mine to Connecticut. Steven and another soldier in his company who lived in Connecticut didn't want to drive to Vermont from Indiana only to drive back to Connecticut. It seemed like a big waste of time. So, Steven, the other soldier from his unit, and I got plane tickets from Cincinnati to Connecticut. We stayed overnight in a hotel near the airport and got to go out for a few beers that night. After a month or so of training, it was nice to have a little bit of freedom.

Being home for Christmas was a big morale boost for me. It allowed me to spend a few more days with my new son, Vicki, and the rest of the family. We managed to fit in a christening for our son during this time too. It wasn't easy to fit in at that time of year, given that Christmastime is one of the church's busier times. Given the circumstances that I wouldn't be back home for over a year, our local church made it happen. Steven, and his fiancée Leeza were Godparents.

After Christmas, Steven and I flew back to Indiana to wrap up any remaining pre-deployment training and paperwork we needed to do. After saying our goodbyes to our family, Steven and I boarded the plane. While we were standing in the rampway to get onto the plane, he started getting choked up. It was emotional for me too, and I was sad to be leaving my wife and newborn son, but it didn't move me to tears. I slapped him on the back and busted his balls for turning on the waterworks. In hindsight, the difference between his reaction and mine had more to do with his combat experience in Iraq. His unit saw a lot of action during that deployment, and he knew people who were injured and even killed. He probably realized that this could be the last time either of us saw our family.

On the drive back to Camp Atterbury from the airport, Steven told me that he didn't have to go on this deployment. His enlistment would end while we were in Afghanistan, so his unit wasn't going to make him deploy just to send him home partway through. He said that he didn't want to see any of the guys he served with in Iraq go to Afghanistan without him. Had something happened to any of them, he might not be able to forgive himself. The unit also had many new soldiers since the Iraq deployment, and he felt a responsibility to lead them. He told me that he chose to reenlist to go on this deployment.

On the day my unit left Camp Atterbury, we had a hectic schedule and missed our unit's scheduled dinner time slot. A few of us snuck away to the chow hall to grab a bite to eat before getting on the bus for the 15-hour bus ride to Ft. Polk in Louisiana. It was a coincidence that it happened to be the same time that Steven's unit was in the chow hall. I managed to grab a seat with Steven and his squad and have what I assumed to be the last meal I'd be able to have with him before I left. This meal was significant because I knew it was the last time I would see any family before getting to Afghanistan. We would not cross paths at Ft. Polk since his unit had already been through JRTC (Joint Readiness Training Center). Little did I know that this meal would also be the last time I saw Steven alive.

Steven got in a few good jokes at my expense in front of the guys in his unit. I had an assault pack stuffed with as much stuff as I could fit in it, plus a few things clipped to the outside. Steven joked that "it looked like it's the first time the little Boy Scout had to go off and play Army." He always found the chink in your armor, but it was all in good fun.

After eating, we boarded our bus to head down to Louisiana. Ft. Polk is in the bottom 2–3 places I've ever been in the world, and I've been to a war zone. We no longer had the luxury of barracks. Instead, our entire company stayed in one enormous tent. For us to all fit, our cots had to be no more than about six inches apart from each other. There was only enough room to do a side step shuffle between each cot. The proximity meant you had someone else very close to the left, right, head, and foot of your rack. So people could walk by without tripping, everything you had needed to fit under the cot.

It also rained almost every day. On one "dry" day, our platoon decided that we would train some of the younger guys how to navigate while driving the HMMWV (pronounced "Humvee"). Our Platoon Leader decided to take us on a trail that went through the woods. Since the rain had soaked the ground, our heavy Humvees sunk in the mud. If we came across an obstacle in the road, the lead vehicle usually dictates whether we could continue. On this particular drive, the lead vehicle's Truck Commander (TC) decided that the standing water on the dirt road "wasn't deep enough" for us to get stuck in. He decided to press on. It turns out he was wrong, and that first truck got stuck in the mud.

We had a few axes with us and chopped down some trees to put under the tires, which gave us enough traction to push that truck through. You'd think this would have been enough to encourage us all to turn around and head back or find a drier route. But we charged on and proceeded to get every single vehicle stuck and unstuck many times. We passed the point of no return and kept moving forward, often forgoing the trail for driving through the woods where the ground was a little more firm. We had radioed for an Army wrecker truck to help pull us out, but they got stuck too and never reached us. I would bet that the woods around that trail are still recovering from the devastation we inflicted. We found a small footbridge about the size of a kitchen table, which we took apart to use the planks to wedge under tires. At that point, we could have been on private property, for all I know. The map we had didn't clearly define property lines, and this bridge looked a little too nice for Ft. Polk.

We started this exercise a little after dinner time, and we were only supposed to be out for an hour or two. We ended up returning about 18 hours later, close to lunchtime the next day. As much as that night sucked, our entire platoon bonded closer together over this shared suffering. Looking back, I wouldn't trade that night for the "comfort" of our cots and the warmth of the tent.

In another rain-plagued training exercise, we slept in our vehicles. There is a hole in the roof of Humvees, where the gunner can man a roof-mounted machine gun. The rain that night was heavy and coming into the Humvee through the gunner's turret. Our gunner draped his poncho over the hole, which kept most of the rain out--except for the one spot that was funneling down on me. I didn't notice it until I woke up the following day and was thoroughly soaked. The morning temperature was about 40-45 degrees, which doesn't sound too cold unless your clothes are soaked. During the day, it only warmed up to about 50 degrees. We continued our training mission, and I looked forward to getting out of the truck and moving around to dry off and warm up.

At some point during the training mission, I started to feel disoriented and began slurring my speech. I told one of my buddies, "I'm having a real-world problem. Something isn't right." He called for a medic, who determined that I had hypothermia when he recorded my temperature at 93 degrees. They took me to a small hospital where I was stripped of my wet clothes and covered in about a dozen heated blankets to bring up my core temperature. After a few days, more warm blankets, and hot meals, I finally felt like myself again. Although, to this day, I can't stand being wet and cold at the same time. I will rarely even go into a swimming pool because the feeling of being in wet clothes makes my skin crawl.

Once we completed our time at Ft. Polk, we traveled to a nearby airport late at night. This trip was different from your typical family vacation or business trip. We sat in a big open room with all our weapons on bleacher-type benches as if we were about to watch a basketball game. We had to put a zip-tie style tag on our rifles, pistols, grenade launchers, and shotguns to show that they were free of ammunition. When it was time to get on the plane, everything, including our weapons, came on board the plane with us.

It was a commercial airplane that the military had chartered to take us out of the United States, so it felt bizarre to be bringing weapons on board. Here we were, several hundred soldiers carrying rifles, shotguns, and pistols all on a regular commercial plane. Instead of putting a briefcase or backpack under the seat in front of us, we had guns—lots of them. Everyone on the flight was a soldier except for the pilots and flight attendants, so don't worry. If you're on your way to Disney World, a soldier won't plop down in the seat next to you with his M-4.

The oddest part about this trip, though, was that we got on the plane, having no idea where in the world it would land. Our chain of command didn't tell us what our exact destination would be for security purposes. If we didn't know where we were going, we weren't able to tell our loved ones where we were going. Then they couldn't accidentally talk about our travel path with some terrorist eavesdropping.

On February 7, 2010, our flight had a layover in Leipzig, Germany. That happened to be Super Bowl Sunday, so our Sergeant Major allowed each of us to have two beers in the terminal as we waited for the plane to get refueled. He should have known that a bunch of grunts couldn't count. Most of us had an armful of booze standing in line at the shop in the airport, with the game playing in the lounge, which made for a fun night in Germany. I only wish I remembered more of it!

Our next flight left the same way our last one did——with us having no idea exactly where our flight would land. We knew it would take us one step closer to where we needed to be in Afghanistan, but we weren't sure exactly where that would be. It turns out this time we landed in Manas, Kyrgyzstan, where we stayed for a few days until the final leg of the trip to Afghanistan. We landed at Bagram Air Base.

Bagram was where I first stepped into Afghanistan, and it was nothing like what I was expecting a war zone to be. The transient holding barracks were relatively comfortable. It was far better accommodations than what we had at Ft. Polk only a few days earlier. The base felt more like a city with paved roads and street signs. There were a variety of fast-food restaurants in addition to the standard military DFAC. There was even a Harley Davidson dealership and a place to buy an Afghan cell phone.

The cell phones there were very cheap compared to what was available to us back home. Granted, the service or the phones weren't always the best quality. Many of us picked one up to communicate with each other while we might be off on different parts of the base.

After a couple of days living it up at Bagram, we flew on to Jalalabad Air Base. Jalalabad is a scaled-down version of Bagram. It didn't have all the luxuries that Bagram had, but it wasn't too bad either. I was starting to think that if this is what Afghanistan was going to be like, maybe it wouldn't be so bad.

I should note, though, that both bases at Bagram and Jalalabad came under attack several times during my deployment. On one occasion, I was in charge of a convoy to Jalalabad on a supply run when the base got attacked. Just because those bases had some luxuries didn't mean that they were immune to attacks.

Finally, we got flown on Chinook helicopters to our final destination, Forward Operating Base (FOB) Torkham.

4

Afghanistan

WE ARRIVED AT FOB TORKHAM late at night. Considering we never were at that base before, we couldn't tell whether we were in a safe area as we got off the helicopters. There was very little light other than the moonlight. It was a little nerve-wracking at first because the layout of the landing area made it look like we were standing out in the open outside the wire. A tall wall of HESCO barriers made up the FOB's inner perimeter. The gate in front of us made it appear like we were standing in the open.

HESCO barriers are enormous sandbags that are stacked up to form a tall barrier. As we exited the helicopter, it appeared as if we were entering the base from outside the wire. Later we found out that we landed inside an outer perimeter, which was a little further out from the main base area.

Our primary mission in Afghanistan was to provide border security. FOB Torkham was about two miles from the Afghanistan/Pakistan border. The crossing at Torkham was one of the most used border crossings for cargo going in and out of Afghanistan. Many individual travelers would cross between the two countries for personal visits.

The Durand Line is the 1,640-mile border between the two countries, which came from an agreement between the British Indian and Afghan governments during the 1890s. The line follows the geography of the land while ignoring the tribal makeup of the area, passing straight through several tribal regions.

If you lived in the area when the governments created the line, you might have found yourself on the Afghan side of the border. Your other family members and neighbors might have ended up on the Pakistani side. All your life up to that point, you could freely visit people who are now on the other side of this border. You likely wouldn't want to change your routine, so you probably would ignore the line. People who inhabit the area to this day still view the line as artificial and meaningless.

To give you an idea of what this was like to the people living there, think about this. Say someone knocked on your door one day, walked in, and drew a line down the middle of your kitchen. The side to the left would be part of a new country, *Refrigeratoria*. The side to the right would be part of another country, *Microwaveistan*. Due to this new border, you would no longer be able to take your leftovers out of the fridge and heat them in the microwave without a passport.

This example seems ridiculous, but I'm guessing there is no chance that you would recognize that border, right? Well, that's pretty much how the local populace views the border between the two countries. Artificial and meaningless.

You can see why there would be a lot of "frequent fliers" traveling between the countries. Many of them didn't appreciate the delays we would cause when they were only trying to visit family on the other side of the border. We would pull a random sample of travelers aside for screening. We would use a screening device that compared various biometric markers to a biometrics database consisting of data collected from known terrorists. If we found any matches, we would detain them on the spot for questioning.

There was also a paved road crossing where we only allowed vehicle traffic to pass through. We would park our trucks on opposite sides of this road crossing - one facing east and the other west. The two trucks made a machine gun face in either direction, making drivers think twice about speeding through the checkpoint.

On one occasion at the border, a kid between 10-12 years old stood up in the back of a "jingle truck" (a brightly decorated dump truck). As it passed through our border crossing checkpoint, I noticed the kid. He pointed what looked like an AK-47 at some of our soldiers as he stood up.

I was only 50-75 meters away, so I raised my rifle to shoot him before he shot the soldiers. As I focused my ACOG rifle sight on the child, I realized he was only holding a piece of wood shaped like a rifle. I decided that there wasn't an immediate threat, so I lowered my weapon.

As I was lowering it, I realized that my safety was off. I had started to squeeze the trigger before concluding that the kid was only carrying a piece of wood. That realization took its toll on me. A few minutes earlier, I believed myself to be the type of person who would do anything to protect children. Yet there I was, with only a few pounds of pressure standing in the way of a bullet ripping through his chest.

On another occasion, an older man started walking through the vehicle road crossing. I started yelling at him to turn around and walk on the pedestrian pathway. When he kept walking, I had my interpreter make sure the message was getting through. When that didn't work, I raised my rifle and pointed it at him. He continued walking.

We had an escalation of force rule that required us to "shout, show, shove, shoot." The 4S's, as we called them, means that we first have to shout to make sure the person knows what we are expecting of them. Next, if they don't respond to the shouting, we have to show our weapons. Showing our weapons means pointing them in the person's direction. If they don't react to having a soldier aiming at them, we're supposed to shove them back. Finally, if none of that deescalated the situation, we would be clear to shoot.

After "showing" or aiming my weapon at the man, I realized that something wasn't right with him. I couldn't place it, but I knew the shouting wasn't getting through to him. While I would have been within my rights to shove or even shoot him, I decided to take a different approach. Rather than getting physical with him, I radioed for all traffic to stop so I could escort him through to the other side.

Later, I found out from the Afghan National Directorate of Security (NDS) agents we worked with that he was both deaf and mentally handicapped. The NDS is an Afghan intelligence agency, approximately equivalent to the US Department of Homeland Security.

I continue to replay the situations with the kid and the old man repeatedly in my head even today. Both made me realize that I was the type of person capable of taking another person's life— even the life of a child or a harmless old man.

The other part of our mission was to ensure that supplies from allied countries could enter the country without delay. Most of the supplies for the US and other NATO (North Atlantic Treaty Organization) countries would travel to Afghanistan on cargo boats. Since Afghanistan is a landlocked country, the cargo had to get offloaded at the closest port in Karachi, Pakistan. Afterward, the containers would get trucked about 1,000 kilometers to Afghanistan via the border crossing at Torkham. From there, they would continue to wherever the final destination was. Our job was to count these trucks to get an estimate of how many made it to Afghanistan. Additionally, we were there as a show of force to the Pakistanis, who often would shut down the border in response to US drone strikes in their country. When a US military presence was there, they tended to keep it open.

Stationed at FOB Torkham was the entirety of Charlie Company 1/102nd Infantry plus various supporting units. Our company consisted of three platoons of regular infantry along with a mortar platoon. Supporting elements included mechanics, cooks, medics, and a few others who I never got to know. The infantry platoons would rotate weekly between three main jobs. One platoon was always working "the gate," as we referred to the border crossing. Another would be performing base security, and a third served as the Quick Reaction Force (QRF). The platoon on QRF duty would have a lighter workload but would be "on-call" should any other platoons need help. Despite being lighter workload, when QRF got called, it usually was because of a more dangerous situation.

Over time, our leadership saw us as more effective when QRF wasn't waiting for something to happen. The platoons on QRF evolved to doing more patrol missions around our area of operations (AO). We would go out on "goodwill" missions to the villages near our base. The goal was to get the villagers on our side to warn us of attacks or Taliban movement through the area. These missions usually stayed within a few miles of our base, so we would still be available to support the other platoons. However, they sometimes would send us out much further. Several times, we did the 80-mile round trip supply runs to Jalalabad. The long journey meant that there was a 40-mile stretch of road where the Taliban could ambush us.

One stretch of this road had a row of low tree branches. In our briefings, we learned that in the past, the Taliban would tie wire across these low tree branches alongside the road. The purpose of the wire was to decapitate our gunners while we passed through. We managed to pass through the area without incident.

On one QRF mission, we responded to a report from villagers who found grenades from a rocket-propelled grenade (RPG) weapon nearby. The grenades lying on the road weren't the dangerous part. It was not knowing who put them there or whether they had rigged it to detonate. Enemy fighters may have even placed them there to lure us to that location for an ambush. Or they could have been drawing us away from the base so they could attack the base while blocking QRF from getting back. We secured the area and waited for the explosive ordnance disposal (EOD) folks to come and remove the grenades. The guys who showed up were civilian contractors driving an up-armored SUV. One of them walked over to the grenades, picked them up, and tossed them in the trunk of his car before driving off. I concluded that he was either suicidal, had balls of steel, or had seen enough of these to know how to handle them.

Another time my platoon was on the QRF rotation, several nomads came and asked us for help to rescue their cows. The cows got caught in a flash flood and huddled together on a small island. Previously, that small island was part of an open field. The space they were standing on was getting smaller by the minute.

We had no idea how we'd save the cows, but we went with the people to see what we could do. We couldn't win the "hearts and minds" if we didn't at least try to help. The floodwaters were moving so fast that we couldn't wade out to the cows. Driving our trucks through the water was out of the question too. The water was much too high and moving far too fast.

Even if we did make it across to the cows somehow, what would we do with them? If we could somehow get them to swim across the moving water, they'd likely get swept away.

Unfortunately, the best bet for those cows' survival was staying put and hoping that the water wouldn't rise much higher. We decided that there wasn't anything we could do to help the cows without risking our lives or equipment. We left shortly after determining that we wouldn't be able to help.

Sticking around to see what happened wouldn't have been very safe for us either. The floodwater was traveling past the base of a mountain, which would have provided a great vantage point for an enemy sniper to start picking us off.

My Squad Leader told me that he was nominating me for the Audie Murphy Award during the early summer months of 2010. This award is an elite award for non-commissioned officers (NCOs) who deserve special recognition.

During the deployment, I was a fire team leader. Fire teams usually consist of four soldiers, a team leader (me), rifleman, grenadier, and automatic rifleman. On paper, I was responsible for three other soldiers.

In reality, I would often find myself stepping up to the squad leader's position, a job reserved for one rank higher than my own. My responsibility would then be for nine soldiers in total, including me. I even stepped into the platoon sergeant's position for a time, a job reserved for two ranks above my own. At that point, I was responsible for about 40 soldiers. I also stepped in as the platoon leader, which is usually a lieutenant's job. I was responsible for a lot of our platoon's administrative paperwork on top of my regular duties. And I would often be in charge of our patrols and our work at the border. Frequently these missions would require me to be responsible for 30+ soldiers and civilians. Some of these people would be VIPs, that we would provide a security detail. These VIPs included several generals and admirals, as well as DOD civilians. Warren Buffet's grandson was one of those DOD civilians.

I'm not listing all of these responsibilities to pat myself on the back. Instead, I'm listing them to give a glimpse into why my Squad Leader considered me for this award.

By all means, it is quite an honor to be considered for an award like this.

And at any point during my time in the Army, the nomination would have been an honor. But this wasn't any other time. I was in Afghanistan.

When my Squad Leader first nominated me for the Audie Murphy Award, I didn't know what the award even was. I knew who Audie Murphy was, but I never knew there was an award bearing his name.

Audie Murphy was the most decorated American soldier during WWII. He received the Medal of Honor for single-handedly holding off a company of German soldiers in 1945 before leading a successful counterattack while wounded and out of ammo. He is legendary not only in the US Army, but ordinary civilians know of him and his heroics as well.

My Squad Leader told me that I would no longer perform my regular duty to give me time to study for the board that I would have to appear before.

Not being able to do my job rubbed me the wrong way. I didn't come to the other side of the world, miss most of the first year of my newborn son's life, and risk my life to get paraded around in front of some board. I could have done that when we were back home, but as far as I knew, our unit hadn't put people up for the award while we were at home. At least not since I became an NCO.

Plus, my platoon would be down a man while I was studying and at the board. Someone else would have to pick up the slack and work my shifts. Meanwhile, I would be on the base hitting the books studying like I was back in college. If something had happened to any of our guys while I was sitting on my ass preparing for the board, I don't know if I'd be able to live with myself.

I brought up my objections to my Squad Leader and Platoon Sergeant. I told them that I wanted them to nominate someone else. Or, preferably, no one at all. They denied my request. I had a pretty good relationship with both my Squad Leader and Platoon Sergeant. Still, they got pretty heated with me after I persisted in my objections. They ended up ordering me to stay on base and study, so that's what I did.

The day I was to appear before the board, I flew off to FOB Mehtar Lam with my Squad Leader and a few other soldiers. I knew that this board was one of many I would have to go through to get the award - kind of like a playoff tournament. If I passed this board, I would go to another board sometime in the future, and who knows how many more after that one. In my head, there was no way I was going to let myself sit around and waste time studying in Afghanistan any longer. I made up my mind that I was going to bomb the board.

When I walked into the room, a few soldiers sat behind a table to administer the board to me. It reminded me of the judges on a TV game show. They started with a few softball questions, which I answered correctly. With each question, I showed some level of hesitation. As if I had to think hard about the answer. Then I decided to bomb a few easy questions to ensure I didn't get selected to move on to the next round.

One question asked what the Army Regulation was that covers the wear and appearance of army uniforms. Every soldier knows the answer is AR 670-1. It's drilled in your head early on in basic training. With a softball question like that, I should have had no problem answering it. Instead, I responded with the wrong number, "AR 583-2", or something along those lines. I swear you could have heard my Squad Leader's jaw hit the ground in disbelief. I glanced over at him with a look like, "See, I told you not to send me."

I know some people won't agree with my reasoning for throwing the board like that. Think of that decision what you will. Receiving the nomination for the award was a pretty incredible honor. I was sidelined for so long that it was tearing me up inside so much. Even if I did well at the board, I wasn't so sure that I'd even want the award. The guys in my platoon were more important to me than any award ever will be, and I just wanted to get back to doing my job.

After a few more quick questions, they dismissed me, and I was on my way back to our base to reunite with our platoon. Finally, I could get back to the job I was there to do.

Back at the FOB, we escorted high-ranking military and DOD civilians to the Pakistani border. These missions were considered personal security detachment (PSD) missions. Essentially, we were the bodyguards for our guests.

After a little while, these missions started becoming boring. Every time we went out, it would be the same. We would meet our VIPs and brief them on where we were going and what to expect. Then we would drive out to our destination and secure the area before they were allowed to exit the vehicles. We would assign several soldiers to form a 360-degree perimeter around the VIPs. They'd walk around, shake hands with local Afghan officials, take some pictures, and then we'd leave.

It would happen this way every single time.

One time we decided to have fun with one of these PSD missions. Some of our guys printed out a bunch of fliers for a fictitious sightseeing company called *Torkham Tours*. It highlighted all of the great features of the Afghan/Pakistani border in a highly sarcastic tone. They included features like the "fine dining" establishments, which in addition to providing you with flatbread and beans, would also give you the shits for a week. The fliers also cautioned our guests against going near the large building that housed the X-Ray equipment that examined the contents of vehicles passing through the border. It's not that the building wasn't interesting (it was). It's just that it emitted high amounts of radiation. We were just looking out for the safety of our guests. We put the fliers with some snacks and water bottles on each VIP's seat so they would know what to expect.

The no-bullshit admiral who was one of our VIPs that day did not think this was very funny. We all got reamed out a bit, and the admiral told us to remove all the fliers and other shit from the vehicles. That was the end of our brief entry into the sightseeing business.

I still say *Torkham Tours* could have survived with a better marketing department.

We had some strange encounters at the border too.

We noticed a man crossing into Afghanistan from Pakistan who stuck out like a sore thumb in early June. He appeared paler than I am, with a shaved bald head and face, wearing western-style clothes and sunglasses. Every other person we ever saw crossing the border had a dark complexion and hair, usually had a beard, and wore traditional Afghan clothing. We referred to the men's clothing as "man-jams." This guy would not have looked out of place walking down Main Street, USA, but he did here.

We pulled this unusually pasty man aside and asked him who he was and what he was doing there. To our surprise, he spoke perfect English. Not only wouldn't he look out of place on Main Street, USA, but he also wouldn't sound out of place either.

He claimed to be an Afghan and was trying to get to his village. When we searched his belongings, we found a receipt for a Western Union wire transfer from a store in Las Vegas. He admitted to being in the United States but insisted that he was an Afghan.

I was genuinely concerned for the guy at that point. Despite what he told me, he wasn't an Afghan. If he was, his family lineage was more likely European, not from any central Asian nation. It felt wrong to send him on his way as he'd likely get murdered by the Taliban in no time. Since he looked so out of place, I thought that maybe he was an American who had escaped from some terrorist group and might need help. Perhaps he worked for the CIA or some other government agency. His story about being an Afghan was complete bullshit.

I radioed back to our Tactical Operations Center (TOC) to figure out what we were supposed to do with this guy. Our FOB had a portion of the base that was closed off to us regular infantry guys. We called it the *secret squirrel base*. A handful of people there were either Special Forces, CIA or some other clandestine organization.

A couple of these *secret squirrels* came out to the border to interrogate the man. After about a half-hour of interrogation, they told us to let him go. We didn't get an explanation as to who he was or what he was doing, and I suspected that this guy might have been a *secret squirrel* himself.

Later that night, my Platoon Sergeant came to me and told me that someone from the US State Department had contacted our FOB. The State Department said that they were looking for the guy we had at the border, and the next time we saw him, we should detain him.

A few weeks later, he showed up at the border again. I only caught a quick glimpse of him as he ducked into the passport office, but it was enough that I knew it was him. I rushed into the office and grabbed him out of line to interrogate him again. This time I radioed the TOC and told them that I had the person the State Department was interested in and wanted them to call back to figure out what we should do with him.

There must have been a changing of the guard at the State Department because, at that time, no one knew who this guy was. We sat there with him all night long - hours after we were supposed to have wrapped up our mission to the border. Eventually, as the sun rose, the TOC told us to cut him loose and return to base.

"Fuck," I thought. I just wasted hours sitting outside the wire, leaving my guys exposed to potential danger for nothing. I swore at that point if I ever saw this guy again, I'd beat the answers I wanted out of him. I never saw him again.

In early August 2010, the patrol missions required us to temporarily move to FOB Zio Haq. It was here that we would stage our missions during much of August. There, we started supporting and training the Afghan army soldiers. The goal was to get them to be able to fight the Taliban on their own. The idea was that if we teach them to fight, our soldiers wouldn't need to be there in the future. When we would go out on missions, we would work alongside the Afghan army, with the Afghans taking the lead. Think of it like we were the driver's ed instructors, and they were the students at the wheel. The student could gain confidence, but we were in charge and could put on the brakes if things got out of hand.

This dual mission with the Afghan Army had been frustrating. They were supposed to be the primary force there, and one of our objectives was to train them to be self-sufficient. The NATO-led International Security Assistance Force (ISAF) wanted to equip them to fight the Taliban independently, reducing their reliance on NATO. Their army at the time consisted of little more than volunteers with uniforms and weapons, and their previous training and discipline were virtually non-existent. For the past few days, we trained one particular unit of Afghan soldiers, and it was tough to keep their collective attention.

During this time was Ramadan, which to Muslims is a month of fasting, among other practices. The fasting takes place from sunrise to sunset and is mandatory for all adult Muslims. The Muslims with us included all the

Afghan soldiers we were training and our interpreters. The practice of fasting prohibited them from eating, drinking, and the use of tobacco products. The training we were running was physically demanding, and summer in Afghanistan can reach temperatures of over 120°F.

The soldiers weren't very eager to train on an empty stomach with little or no chance of eating or drinking until sundown. We would get them to practice with us for about an hour a day at most before they started wandering off to find the comfort of the shade. It was like herding cats at times.

The training would have been worse if we delayed it until nighttime. That is when Muslims finally get to eat and drink. There is no doubt that they would have ignored us during their nightly feast. Plus, the Afghans lacked the night vision equipment we had, so they couldn't see what they were doing very well.

We had no restrictions on what we could eat or drink, but we didn't want to rub it in their faces either. We tried to eat and drink out of sight from them as much as possible. We did our best, but it didn't seem like they were very interested in the training. Some were also high on opium or other drugs, making it even more challenging to get their attention. The lack of training made it difficult for us to hand over Afghanistan's security to the Afghans themselves. That was above my paygrade, though.

Between training sessions, we would plan out our next mission. We had to ensure we had the resources and personnel needed to complete the mission and rehearse the mission ourselves. Regardless of whether the Afghans wanted to work, we made sure we prepared as much as possible.

All the missions conducted during this time were air assault missions. Air assault missions involve the use of helicopters to transport troops to and from wherever our missions were. We would leave at night under cover of darkness because it was usually safer to land a helicopter that the enemy couldn't see. However, we usually landed close enough to the villages that the enemy could hear the helicopters as they landed. Unfortunately, I suspect that this gave the enemy a chance to escape on more than one occasion.

The Afghan army didn't have night vision goggles, so we would wait until the sun rose before moving off the landing zone. We would land on nearby mountaintops to take advantage of the high ground, so walking down the mountain into the villages was easy. The climb out of the villages was a different story.

On one occasion, we had a peaceful mission where no one fired a shot, including our M-240B machine gunner. The M-240B machine gun itself weighs around 28 pounds. Plus, there were about 1,000 rounds of ammunition, which weigh approximately 40 pounds. Add to that the weight of the standard Kevlar helmet and vest, and our machine gunner was easily carrying over 100 pounds.

As we were climbing back up the mountain, he had about enough of carrying all that ammo and handed it off to another member of our platoon. After the other guy took it a little way up the mountain, he quit too and handed it to me to carry up the rest of the way. Even I had to stop carrying it because I couldn't go any further with it. The mortarmen who had spent all day at the top of the mountain were able to come down and retrieve the ammo for us. At one point, I was starting to hope someone would start shooting at us so we could dump the ammo in their direction, but we had no such luck.

While the weight of the ammo was a factor, it wasn't the only reason it was so difficult to carry. We had practiced carrying heavier weight when we did "buddy carries," which simulated carrying an injured soldier. The load wasn't the problem. FOB Torkham, our base for most of the deployment, was about 2,500 feet above sea level. These missions were operating at well over 10,000 feet in elevation. The problem was that our bodies did not have time to acclimate to this higher elevation.

Regardless of your fitness level, unless you've acclimatized to that altitude, you can't operate at your peak level. At roughly 10,000 feet in elevation, your body will experience reduced physical performance. You'll also have some psychological effects, including decreased judgment and altered mood. The decreased judgment might explain why I wanted someone to start shooting at us to dump some ammo.

5

August 22, 2010

AUGUST 22, 2010, WAS A TYPICALLY HOT, sweltering day in Afghanistan. The mission we were on that day had started late the night before. Our mission was to raid a remote village where we believed the Taliban to be hiding out. The intelligence we gathered indicated that the Taliban might have stolen Afghan Army uniforms and weapons. Since we were on a joint mission with the Afghan Army, the Taliban using Afghan Army uniforms was a problem. If the good guys we were with and the bad guys we were looking for are wearing the same uniforms, who do you shoot? We convinced the legitimate Afghan Army soldiers to wear white armbands on the mission. We told them that we would assume anyone wearing an Afghan Army uniform without an armband is Taliban and would get shot. That convinced the legitimate Afghan soldiers to keep their armbands tied tight.

This mission that day was an air assault mission, which we had done several times in the weeks leading up to this mission. Air assault is considered the movement of friendly assault forces by rotary-wing aircraft to engage and destroy enemy forces or seize and hold key terrain. In the areas we were operating in, the rugged terrain wouldn't allow our MRAP (Mine-Resistant Ambush Protected) trucks to get us to the village. It was also too far away for us to be able to walk there.

The night before, our unit took off in several CH-47 Chinook helicopters and landed on the top of the mountain just to the East of the village.

I had flown in Chinook helicopters before and was familiar with getting on and off safely. When getting off, you are supposed to wait for the rear door gunner to give you the okay to exit because they're in communication with the other crew. Waiting is also necessary because wearing night-vision goggles causes you to lose some depth perception. A lack of depth perception makes it more challenging to determine your height from the ground. On that night, after getting the signal from the rear door gunner that it was okay to begin exiting the helicopter, I stepped off the back, expecting my foot to touch the ground immediately. Instead, while wearing 100+ pounds of gear, I fell three to four feet onto uneven terrain and twisted my knee. I was in pain, but the sun would come up in a few short hours, and I had a mountain to descend and soldiers to lead. I needed to focus on the mission and look past that pain.

The remainder of that night was spent quietly on top of the mountain, pulling security to ensure that nobody from the village snuck up on us. A few hours later, we made our way down into the village at first light to conduct our mission searching for the Taliban fighters.

The Afghan soldiers took the lead on this mission, and they did most of the work searching houses. However, we were also there to support them should they encounter any resistance. When they would discover evidence of Taliban activity, like stolen Afghan Army uniforms or weapons, we would destroy it. We burned the uniforms so that they wouldn't be used by the Taliban again. With our attached EOD soldiers, any weapons and other contraband that wouldn't burn so quickly were strapped to some C-4 explosives and blown up.

At one point, because I was concerned about alerting the Taliban, I radioed for permission to silence a dog that was barking outside as we approached a house. I remembered Steven telling me that they would frequently shoot the wild dogs barking at them in Iraq. The idea was that they didn't want the dog's bark to alert the nearby enemy. I guess gunfire in Ramadi in 2006 was more common than a dog's bark. That's why I thought it might be a good idea to silence this dog.

My Platoon Sergeant denied my request because I would have had to shoot the dog or use my knife to silence it. Shooting the dog would have drawn even more attention to us, considering that there wasn't any gunfire in the village up until that point. Using my knife would have unnecessarily risked getting bitten by the dog, which could have been carrying disease. In that case, it was better to leave the dog alone.

While we were approaching the far end of the village, I received word that my squad needed to secure a landing zone for a helicopter. It wasn't clear who would be landing there, but I knew whoever it was probably was important. Your average Joe doesn't just drop in on a mission unannounced.

I led my squad to create a 360-degree perimeter around a flat clearing on the outskirts of the village. When the helicopter landed, a US Army General and several French soldiers exited. Since this village was in French-controlled territory, I suspected the French soldiers were there to check on the status of the mission. Being the senior-ranking soldier at the landing site, I greeted them as they exited the helicopter. I led them over to the village where we were finishing up our operations. As we were walking, I made small talk with the General. While we were talking, he had received word on his radio that there were two American casualties in another part of Afghanistan. I felt terrible about it, but there wasn't much I could do for them. The General started sharing the few details that he had at the time, but he didn't know their names or where it took place. Eventually, my Platoon Sergeant took over for me. I led my squad back into the village, where our Afghan counterparts were continuing to clear buildings.

Later that afternoon, I heard a call on the radio. "Three-One (my radio call sign), Crusader-Six (the commander's call sign) is looking for you." I couldn't wrap my head around why the commander would want to speak with me. That kind of thing only happens when you do something either really well or very poorly. I had done my job that day and couldn't think of anything extraordinary that had happened to make me stand out. I racked my brain to figure out what I had screwed up.

Then, it occurred to me that maybe one of my guys messed up. Perhaps they had lost a sensitive item, and the commander found it. Sensitive items are military terminology for weapons, night-vision goggles, weapon sights, or other equipment marked with a serial number. I started checking all of my soldier's equipment to ensure they had it all. I even had a small notebook I carried everywhere with me with all the gear my soldiers were issued and the serial numbers for each item. My inspection discovered that they had everything they were supposed to have. I couldn't figure out why the commander was looking for me.

I was at the bottom of the hill at the time of this impromptu inspection. The commander was at the top, so I began to work my way up after doing my due diligence. It was slow going because one of my soldiers had rolled his ankle, and I didn't want to injure him further. I was anxious to get to the commander and find out why he wanted to see me. I became frustrated and said to the limping soldier, "If you can't figure out how to get up the mountain, you can stay down here for all I care." I immediately realized that this wasn't one of my finest leadership moments. I ended up asking other soldiers in my squad to help carry his load and get him up the mountain, and then I took off at a faster pace alone. My knee was also still bothering me from my fall earlier in the day, so I ran low on sympathy at that point.

Your mind starts to wander when the commander calls you, and you have no idea what he wants. You want the pain of knowing what he wants to be over as soon as possible, so it creates a bit of unexpected anxiety. These aren't excuses for my behavior or what I said, just the reality of the situation.

As my mind wandered, the thought of getting a Red Cross message entered my head. A Red Cross message is how family members back home can communicate emergency messages to military personnel serving overseas. It is the same as when Vicki had attempted to send a message when she was going into labor. Perhaps something happened to an elderly family member back home. "Had my grandfather passed away or was there some sort of emergency? Maybe something happened to my wife or son," I thought. The suspense was horrible. "Why couldn't he just tell me what he wanted over the radio?"

The people who were up on top of the mountain pointed me in the direction of the commander. The Sergeant Major for our entire battalion approached me and said, "Take off your helmet, come over here and take a knee. With my banged-up knee, that was just about the last thing I wanted to do. I did what he said while thinking to myself, "Something has to be wrong. They never tell you to take off your helmet when you are outside the wire."

The commander sat down next to me. He said, "There's no easy way to say this, but your brother and his unit got ambushed. There was an attack, and your brother got hit." Instantly, my thoughts went to, "OK, he's hurt somewhere and needs my help. Maybe he needs a blood transfusion or a kidney? We're probably the same blood type, but I don't know for sure. Get me on a helicopter to see him. If there is something I have that I don't need, he can have it." I didn't quite comprehend what he meant by saying Steven got hit.

My commander looked at me and said, "He didn't make it." Just then, a wave of emotion came over me. I just completely broke down, which was out of character for me. He put his arm around me in an attempt to comfort me. We sat there for a few minutes while he consoled the sobbing mess I had become.

Neither my commander nor I knew what had happened on the mission where Steven died. He told me that he was sure Steven took out at least a few of the Taliban before they got him to lift my spirits a bit.

When I read the sworn statements that the soldiers in Steven's unit made, I found a few different versions of what happened on the mission. Each soldier's account recalled the events a little differently based on their perspective. However, based on the statements and conversations with the soldiers, we can piece together a pretty accurate picture of what took place that day. Based on about two dozen sworn statements and investigation reports our family received from the Army, here is what happened.

* * *

In Afghanistan, Steven's unit, 3rd Platoon, Alpha Company, 3/172 Infantry, was stationed at Combat Outpost (COP) Herrera. Their mission was to mentor the Afghan Border Police (ABP) and conduct missions in nearby villages.

On August 22, 2010, Steven's company and their Afghan counterparts headed out to the Jaji district, Paktia province, in Eastern Afghanistan. Their mission that morning was to sweep through the area to search for weapon caches and enemy fighters.

The insurgents in the area had been intimidating the local citizens by using violent tactics for a while. It was Steven's unit's mission to clear the enemy out of the district. These enemy fighters had also fired on Steven's unit before, so his unit knew the enemy's capabilities.

Upon leaving COP Herrera, they drove to the village of Roqian, where they dismounted from their vehicles. As they dismounted the vehicles at the beginning of the mission, Steven jumped out and ripped the crotch of his pants. He wasn't wearing any underwear that day, so he turned to his good friend, Wes Black, and said, "Hey, Wes, do you want some bubble gum?" while holding his nuts outside his pants. Apparently, this wasn't the first time Steven had done this to get a laugh out of the soldiers in his platoon, but it was probably the only time he did it while out on a mission.

His unit then moved across a field to the first objective house. The first objective was a three-story building that was known to be a cache site in the past. They cleared this house successfully with no weapons or enemy found and then linked up with the other part of the company.

The terrain in this area was very rugged, with a lot of vegetation. This unforgiving terrain made it difficult for the various elements to stay in line, which is essential to avoid accidentally shooting friendlies. They made due as best as they could with what the terrain offered them.

Steven's platoon was positioned on the left flank of his company as they swept through the village. After the first objective, they moved about 500 meters along the hilltops until they paused to let the lower element, who had more distance to cover, catch up and get back in line. As they began moving again, they got ambushed.

At least four insurgents near Steven's position armed with AK-47s and grenades were supported by a PKM machine gun team about 400 meters away. Another soldier who was a little ways behind Steven saw him run forward towards some small trees for cover. At this point, he had moved forward enough that he passed one of the dead insurgents who had been shooting at them. There was a lot of gunfire going on from both sides. From Steven's position, it wasn't easy to tell what direction the gunfire was originating.

Steven looked back towards the other soldiers in his unit that were a few feet behind him to yell out some instructions. As he started to speak, his head jerked back, and he slumped backward on his assault pack. The soldiers near him yelled for a medic, but the gunfire was so intense that the initial call for a medic went unheard.

Shortly after this initial wave of attack, the incoming fire had slowed to just the occasional shot here and there. The first soldier to reach Steven's position started to hear cracks of machine-gun fire all around him. Before he could continue checking Steven, he needed to return fire to the PKM team engaging him. He fired roughly 50 rounds towards the PKM fire before they broke contact and moved to another position.

No longer receiving fire, he turned to check on Steven for responsiveness. Unfortunately, there was none. It was then that he noticed a small pool of blood underneath Steven's head and neck. He observed an entry wound on Steven's left cheek, and an exit wound out the back of his head near where his head and spine meet. The medic, who had gotten pinned down during the exchange of gunfire, flew up the hill to reach Steven's position. When he arrived, he quickly checked for a pulse and after not finding one, pronounced him dead.

The first soldier to reach Steven was his friend Wes Black, who Steven offered his "bubble gum" to earlier in the day. When he was helping package Steven up to get him off the hill, he noticed that Steven's nuts were hanging out of his pants, which caused Wes to start hysterically laughing. When he realized that all the other soldiers must have thought he was crazy, he pointed at Steven and asked, "You want some bubble gum?" The other soldiers looked at Steven's crotch and erupted in laughter at the situation. They all knew his good sense of humor and agreed that Steven would have wanted them to get one last good laugh from his "bubble gum" antics.

At this point, the mission changed. It was no longer about clearing the insurgents out of the village. It quickly became a recovery mission to get Steven's body off of the mountain.

Part of the Soldier's Creed says *I will never leave a fallen comrade.* Those soldiers worked to do everything they could so that Steven would not get left behind.

A few soldiers gathered at Steven's position. They dragged his body towards a flat spot downhill from where he got shot so he could get loaded onto a pole-less litter for evacuation. Four soldiers picked up his body and moved it downhill towards the landing zone (LZ), where the medevac helicopter would land.

The soldiers moved him about 100 meters when his body started coming loose from the litter. Steven coming loose caused them to stop in an exposed position to readjust his body on the litter. As they placed his body down, gunfire ripped between the litter bearers and the rest of the platoon. RPGs and grenades began exploding throughout Steven's platoon's location, causing everyone to dive for cover.

When the soldiers carrying his body had to put him down, Steven was left exposed in the open. At the same time, the other soldiers in his platoon returned fire from a nearby ditch that provided some cover. They called on their mortarmen to fire at the enemy fighting positions.

During this second ambush, SPC Tristan Southworth got hit and fell into the ditch with the other soldiers. The medic reached him soon after and sat him up to check him for wounds. After an initial search, the medic found one wound in his upper left chest. Due to the massive blood loss that he sustained, and the determination that the damage was not treatable, the medic ceased treatment and pronounced him dead. There were now two American soldiers and one ABP officer killed on this mission and several others wounded.

During a lull in the fighting, the soldiers made their way down the hill towards the closest house they could find to take it for a casualty collection point (CCP). Once they got there, the CCP would also serve as a place for the other wounded and exhausted soldiers to catch their breath for a few minutes.

To get to the CCP, the soldiers needed to move fast. Unfortunately, there wasn't much cover between their position and the CCP, so the soldiers moved Steven and Tristan's bodies down the hill by falling, sliding, rolling, and crawling towards the nearest house. Since there wasn't any cover to hide behind, their best bet was to keep moving since a moving target is more challenging to hit than a stationary one. The faster they got down the hill, the less likely it was that anyone else would get hit. They slid down the rough terrain through thorns, rocks, irrigation ditches, and other obstacles. It wasn't the easiest, but it was all they had available at the time.

As they slid and rolled down the mountain, they came across a house built into the hillside. The soldiers slid Steven and Tristan's bodies onto the house's roof as they approached the house from above. They would use this house as their CCP.

Four soldiers from Steven's platoon then proceeded to clear the house. Inside were two males in one room and several females in another. After securing the building, several soldiers moved Steven and Tristan's bodies to the lower level. There the bodies were stripped of any sensitive items and prepared to be transferred to the LZ.

The company's 1st platoon helped secure the LZ for the medevac helicopter to land. Once it landed, soldiers carried Steven and Tristan's bodies to the LZ. The medevac flew to Bagram, where Steven and Tristan were placed into a transfer case to transport them to Kuwait the next day.

Back at the mission, upon returning to the CCP building, the platoon learned of an enemy force consisting of about 200 fighters headed towards them. Their instructions were to hold at their location and take up defensive positions. Their defensive position would allow the ABP to clear the other two objective houses in the village and defend against the incoming fighters.

Unfortunately, they ran out of daylight at this point. The Afghans did not have night vision goggles as the Americans had, so they refused to continue with the mission. Luckily the warning about the incoming enemy fighters was a false alarm, so 1st and 3rd platoons moved back to their vehicles, which the 2nd platoon secured earlier in the day. The company could not leave the village as they provided security to Charlie Company, who arrived to assist with the mission.

They ended up staying in their trucks for the remainder of the night and finally returned to COP Herrera in the morning at first light.

* * *

While I didn't know any of those details until weeks later, after I had returned home to Connecticut, my mind was imagining what might have happened. Now back on my mission, my commander called a couple of guys from my platoon to stay with me. He had over a hundred American and Afghan soldiers he was in charge of, so he couldn't stay with me for long. I was grateful that he called those guys over because I didn't want to be left alone at that moment.

While I processed what I had just learned, my commander was mindful that I was also sitting there with a loaded rifle and lots of ammunition. As he left, he asked, "Are you okay? You're not going to hurt yourself or anything like that?" I assured him that I was okay in that regard. I was definitely in shock and upset, but not suicidal.

At the time, it made me a little pissed off that he would ask a question like that. He knew I had a wife and a newborn son at home. He knew my parents just lost a son. How the hell could I let them suffer through another loss like that? I realize now why he asked the question, and I am appreciative of it. At the time, though, it just rubbed me the wrong way. As I'd come to learn, a lot of things would rub me the wrong way after this day.

Two sergeants from my platoon stayed with me for about ten minutes. Since they also had other guys to oversee, they called another two guys over. No one wanted to leave me alone for too long. However, within about 20 minutes of learning that my brother had died, we heard gunshots and explosions all around us.

Our unit was receiving small arms and RPG fire from the surrounding village. I was the squad leader of the two soldiers who were now with me, and I was in charge of eight more. I was a wreck, but it was instantly clear that I had to put aside my issues to continue to lead my soldiers against this sudden attack.

As I assessed the situation, I realized we were under fire from both sides of the mountain. I told the guys who were with me to go back down to join the rest of the squad and find a covered position to defend our area. Of course, I had been sitting there without a ballistic helmet, so I ran as best as I could on my injured leg to retrieve it and then back over to where my guys were. We had the high ground, which is easier to defend. However, I was still concerned since bullets were flying in our general direction.

Meanwhile, I had my squad positioned behind the few large rocks that were in the area. Besides that, there was nothing more than a few small rocks, and those would not be enough to provide any protection as positioned. So, we gathered more of the smaller stones and built a lower barrier for cover. What was going through my head as we were under fire was, "I just got the worst news I could imagine, and now I'm dealing with this shit too. And, somehow, I have to make sure my squad is safe and doing the right things." Did we have enough ammunition and cover? Were there any gaps in the area where my guys were covering? Figuring this out while I was also dealing with the emotions of losing my brother was hard. To be honest, at that moment, I was also filled with a lot of anger.

During this attack, an Afghan soldier near me used hand gestures to indicate that his rifle wouldn't shoot. He didn't speak English, and I didn't know much Pashto, but hand gestures are pretty universal. He shook his hand over his weapon the same way you would shake a salt shaker. He was indicating that he needed oil for his rifle. Then he rubbed his hand up and down the length of the weapon, suggesting that he needed a rag to wipe off the dirt.

Got it, message received.

It looked to me like he had never cleaned his weapon before, so it had become jammed with dirt and other debris. As he was motioning to me for some cleaning supplies, I remember thinking, "You are shit out of luck now. I'm not fishing through my stuff to give you cleaning supplies that I'll never get back. Maybe now you'll learn that you should do this before you go out on a mission like we tried to tell you to do!"

Looking back, I can't believe that I didn't even care that he didn't have a functioning rifle. At that point, I was so angry and didn't trust any Afghan, so in my mind, this was just one less Afghan I had to worry about turning his weapon on us.

As I was lying behind those rocks, I heard a couple of gunshots. Our squad's machine gunner said, "Oh shit, I think I see…!" As he trailed off, I said, "Well, why aren't you shooting?" He unloaded bullets in that direction until I told him to stop. I said, "Either you got him, or he ran away. Save your ammo." There was a small structure with no roof on the far side of the valley. Our commander ordered our squad to launch grenades in that direction for fear that someone was hiding behind those walls. One of the guys who had been comforting me earlier was one of my grenadiers. We were pretty good friends, and he was also angry at what had happened to Steven, so he was inclined to unload all of his grenades over there out of pure anger. I also had to tell him to stop and save some. We might need them later. He still directed a lot of fire into that area.

Despite the number of grenades shot out of the M203 grenade launchers, we didn't convince our commander we smoked anyone out. He called in an airstrike on that same position. Fighter jets flew over and obliterated the building like it never existed. Darkly, that felt satisfying at the time. I was kind of happy that I wouldn't have to worry about those people anymore.

After quelling the attack, the commander requested a helicopter to take a few wounded soldiers and me out of the area. As I was on top of the mountain awaiting the helicopter, I went over to my platoon sergeant to turn over my "extra" ammunition and radio. They needed it more than me since they would probably be sitting on top of that mountain for at least a few more hours, if not a few more days. I'd be going to a relatively safe base. I kept one magazine, and I took out a smoke grenade to signal a safe landing point to the helicopter.

As I was waiting for the helicopter, I looked at the Afghan soldiers and our interpreters who were with us. I felt an enormous amount of anger and hatred towards them. I wasn't a hateful person. I even became friends with a few of the interpreters during my time in Afghanistan. Yet here I was, hating them and other people I barely knew. I hated them for not taking care of their own country. And I hated that their country was still a mess despite nine years of American intervention at that time. A messed up country, which made it necessary for people like my brother to come there to die.

As I thought the Black Hawk helicopter was approaching to land, I pulled the pin off the smoke grenade. I was still holding the spoon, which is the little arm at the top that triggers the timer to count down after you let it go. Then, an NCO near the landing zone relayed to me that the helicopter was going to make another pass before landing. I'm standing there holding this grenade, knowing that if my hands slip, I have just a few seconds before it starts billowing smoke right in front of my face. I laughed briefly at the thought of the smoke puffing up in an almost cartoon-like fashion in my face. It would have been a shitty way to end an already terrible day.

As the pilots radioed that the helicopter was going to land, I threw the grenade. Just then, some guys were walking right into the landing zone from the other side. With the smoke, the helicopter pilot likely wouldn't be able to see the soldiers as he was coming down right on top of them. I started screaming at the top of my lungs, warning them to get out of the way. They had leg injuries, so they were hobbling out of the way too slowly for me not to be worried that they would now be suffering a much worse trauma.

Fortunately, they moved in time for the helicopter to land safely. I got on, along with a few other guys.

As I boarded, the General I had encountered earlier was sitting directly across from me on the helicopter. He recognized me and said, "Weren't you the one who I was talking to about those soldiers who got killed?" I said, "Yeah. One of them was my brother." He looked at me like he couldn't believe the coincidence. Out of thousands of other soldiers in Afghanistan at the time, I happened to be the one standing next to him when he first heard the news come in over the radio. He continued to offer his condolences and told me the few details that he knew at the time. He said that he believed one of the soldiers had gotten shot, and the other might have gotten hit by shrapnel from an RPG.

As the Black Hawk soared over the barren Afghan landscape, I kept looking out the door at the random houses we would pass over. I wanted to unload the remaining rounds I had into one of the houses. I knew I couldn't do it without someone on the ground firing at us first, but I sort of wished they would.

We stopped at a medical facility to unload the wounded before heading to Bagram Air Base. Not long after arriving at Bagram Air Base, I turned in all of the equipment I had on me: my M-4 rifle, M-500 shotgun, remaining ammunition, bulletproof vest, helmet, etc. After that, military traditions seemed to go out of the window. It was like they understood my situation and didn't want me to get caught up in customs like addressing an officer as "sir" or "ma'am." I only mention this because you usually get chewed out if you slack on any of these customs. I didn't care at that time, and I think everyone knew it. Moreover, I don't think anyone had it in them to chew out a grieving brother because they were offended that I didn't address them adequately.

There was a chaplain there who spent some time talking with me and giving me spiritual guidance. I honestly don't remember all of what was said, but it felt good to talk to someone openly about what was going on.

The Army also had me speak with a psychiatrist to ensure that I wasn't suicidal and could handle the trip back home. Ultimately, I would be traveling with other soldiers for most of the trip, but not with anyone who knew who I was or what I was going through. She also prescribed something to help me sleep, which I later found to be a blessing on the return flights.

I had met with the Brigade Commander and Sergeant Major in their TOC (Tactical Operations Center). Since most of them were from Vermont, many memorabilia from Vermont were hanging on the walls. One item that nearly caused me to break down and cry again was a Norwich University flag.

I had told the Brigade Commander that I wanted to accompany Steven's body home. He told me they couldn't allow me to do that because his body would get flown to Kuwait first. Steven would remain there for several days before being sent back to The United States. I didn't care. I wanted to stay with him.

"I will never leave a fallen comrade," the line from the Soldier's Creed, is something that got drilled into our heads since the early days of basic training. You never leave a fallen soldier. Ever. How could I wrap my head around leaving my brother behind with a bunch of strangers to look after him?

The Brigade Commander said that if I was to stay with Steven the entire way home, what good would I be doing for him? He was gone, and there was nothing I could do for him. On the other hand, if I was to return home as soon as possible, I could at least be there for my family. My family not only just lost a loved one but also were worried about me. They wanted me home as soon as possible. He also told me that only special operations could escort their fallen home. I thought this was bullshit. I felt like I would be leaving him all by himself like lost luggage.

In the end, the Brigade Commander's logic had convinced me not to keep pushing to escort my brother the entire way home. However, he did say that it might be possible for me to accompany his body out of Afghanistan on the flight to Kuwait. I had to travel to Kuwait on my way home anyway, so this seemed like a fair compromise.

I started to get my mind centered on just getting back home. I wanted to contact my parents and my wife, but I wasn't allowed to call. The officers said they needed to confirm that my parents received the Army's formal death notification. Given the time difference between Afghanistan and the United States East Coast, it was already late at night at our home in Connecticut. No one at the National Guard headquarters in Connecticut could confirm that my parents had received formal notification at that hour. Until we could get confirmation that my parents had received their "knock at the door," I wouldn't be able to call home. It was killing me that I couldn't even call them for five minutes.

A communication blackout is the standard operating procedure anytime there is a military death. All communication back home is cut off, not just for immediate family members like me. Entire units get cut off from calling home. They enact a communication blackout so the deceased's family members don't hear about their loved one's death before getting the official military notification.

After meeting with the Brigade Commander, the Brigade Sergeant Major gave me one of his clean uniforms to wear and some toiletries to clean myself up. I hadn't showered for a couple of days at that point, and I'm sure I smelled pretty gross. My right pant leg had also been completely torn up after my fall from the helicopter earlier that day, so I greatly appreciated the new uniform. The Brigade Sergeant Major was significantly shorter than me, so the sleeves didn't quite make it to my wrists, and the pant legs were just barely long enough to blouse my boots. It wasn't perfect, but it was passable.

As I was taking a shower, I got the first moment alone since learning of

Steven's death. I rested my head against the wall under the showerhead and let the water roll down my back. As I stood there, the tears started rolling down my face, and I shouted, "Why Steve, why?" I would often call him "Steve" when he was alive, and it wasn't until after his death that I began referring to him as "Steven."

I wasn't calling to Steven as if I thought he would hear me and respond to my question. Instead, it was a plea to God to help me understand why he decided that Steven, at only 25 years old, needed to be called to heaven. I wanted to know why He took Steven and not me. Why would my son have to grow up not knowing his Uncle? Why would my parents have to bury a son?

It was at that moment that I realized no answer would be sufficient for me. Even if God himself appeared before me and said Steven needed to die for a particular reason, I don't think I could have accepted it. Instead, I realized that I had to trust that whatever reason God had for taking Steven from us was a good reason. I knew that whatever the reason was, God's plan was good, and that was all I needed to know. Who knows, maybe it was God who put that thought in my head. Perhaps it was my Catholic upbringing. Whatever it was, I felt a relative peace come over me in that shower on Bagram.

The next day, I got asked to be a part of a ramp ceremony for my brother. A ramp ceremony is a memorial service for a fallen soldier held at the airfield before the departure of the aircraft carrying their body. Before returning to our home in Connecticut, Steven's body was first going to Kuwait, then to Dover Air Force Base. Along the way, there would be an investigation into his death, an autopsy, and his body prepared to get sent back home.

I later learned that this ceremony was a big production that they'd rehearsed in the early morning hours. Many high-ranking officials, civilians, and foreign service members would be coming to pay their respects. My role was to stand in a receiving line, much like that of a Catholic wake. The only differences between a wake and a ramp ceremony were that we were standing outside a military cargo plane, and the caskets were metal boxes packed with ice and secured to the aircraft floor. I'm not sure how I was able to hold it together and greet people, except that I was probably still in a state of shock and perhaps in disbelief.

Later, I was waiting in the terminal area of the base, hoping to also get on the same flight to Kuwait as Steven. At the last minute, a spot opened up for me. When I found out I had a seat, I only had a few minutes to get to that C-17. I sprinted to make it, carrying my rucksack weighed down with everything I had. When I got to the plane, I found that everyone was waiting outside the plane, waiting for me to get there first. Typically, you don't get to choose your seat on these types of flights. You just get what you get. Everyone on the flight waited to board to let me choose my seat, so I took the closest to the transfer case that held Steven's body.

As the flight took off, I played out a scenario in my head. I felt like I owed it to him to be right there protecting him. Maybe that's because I wasn't there when he needed me the most. If anyone had tried to touch the transfer case he was in or disrespected it in any way, I would have been all over them like a guard dog.

There is a military tradition of saluting the bodies as they are coming off the plane. When this happens, someone gives the command called "order arms" to end the salute. After we landed in Kuwait, an escort met me and asked if I wanted to have that honor of calling the order arms command out to everyone on the plane. I wasn't sure if I would get too choked up to get the words out. The guy who typically would have done it was standing next to me. He said, "If you don't think you can do it, tap my arm, and I'll do it for you." Well, when the time came, it took me a second to take a deep breath and push through. Just as he was about to take over, I issued the command, and everyone brought their arms down. It was an honor for me to be there for that.

As I landed in Kuwait, a couple of soldiers met me at the airfield to drive me to the Ali Al Salem Air Base, where I'd wait for my next flight. It was slightly different from typical transportation because we went in a civilian car on the main highway. For security purposes, the soldiers and I all took off our uniform blouses and covers. (The Army term for our uniform top is a "blouse," and "cover" is the vernacular for a hat.) Everyone else on the plane got taken on busses to the base. Those busses had window shades pulled down so no one on the outside could tell that the bus was full of soldiers.

While Kuwait is a relatively safe country, there still could be some extremists who would love to get their hands on an unarmed American soldier.

I asked the soldiers who were driving me to the base if they knew whether or not my parents had received notification of my brother's passing. They didn't know, but they led me to the soldier in charge of the passenger terminal when we got to the waiting area. He was already aware of who I was and had contact with the National Guard in Connecticut. He confirmed that my parents had learned what happened the same day Steven died, but it was late at night in their time zone, which is why we didn't find out that they got notified right away. I asked if I could call them and if I could borrow someone's calling card. Several people immediately volunteered theirs. I only took one because I knew I couldn't stay on the phone long and that I could be leaving for my flight at any time.

I called my parents first. I had pictured several officers coming to their door to say that Steven had been killed, then leaving them all alone sobbing in grief. I had been so worried for them, feeling that they must have been anxious to know where I was and how I was doing. We were over 6,000 miles apart, with nothing to connect us but a ten-minute call. I was surrounded by other soldiers, feeling the loneliest I had ever felt in my life. I assured my parents that I was out of danger in Kuwait and would soon be on my way home. I couldn't tell them when I'd be arriving or what path I'd be taking. Even if I knew exactly when I was leaving or where I would be traveling through, which I didn't, I couldn't tell them for security purposes. Not only weren't the phone lines secure, you just never know who my parents might talk to or who might overhear the conversation. As the old saying goes, "loose lips sink ships."

I had about another ten minutes left on the calling card to call my wife. When she answered at around 9:30 a.m. her time, Vicki was driving to my parents' house after packing up our 9-month old son and Roxy (our dog) to stay with them there for a few days. She had heard what happened to Steven the night before from my parents. I told her that I found out before they did, but I couldn't call before the news went through the proper channels. I wanted to see what she needed and make sure she was okay with everything that was happening. I could not do much about it if she needed anything anyway, but I wanted to let her know I was there for her. Vicki assured me that she had spoken with Chaplain Nutt the night before (the Army Chaplain who married us about two years earlier). He had calmed her down by explaining what we should expect. She asked me how I was doing and if I was alone. I said that while I was traveling by myself, I wasn't alone. Meaning that I didn't know anyone traveling with me, but there were plenty of people around. It did feel like I was alone, to be honest. I told her that I had made it safely to Kuwait, but I couldn't give her more information about my journey home for the same reasons I couldn't tell my parents.

Not long after getting notified, my parents had started calling other members of our big family, and those people called more people. My brother's fiancé, Leeza, was told directly by the same chaplain and soldier who had informed my parents of Steven's death earlier that night. When the Army officers approached her door, she thought Steven was there to surprise her with an early return. I guess she was envisioning one of those sappy military homecoming videos on her front doorsteps.

After finishing my calls, I was brought to a transient holding tent with others waiting for up to a week for their flight back home. Some were on leave; others had completed their tours and were heading home for good. A few were in the "family emergency" category like me. I was somehow bumped to the top of the flight list and got on the next flight headed to the United States that same day. No one gets to leave that quickly, but I'm sure the circumstances created a bit more sense of urgency to get me on my way.

6

The Homecoming

THE EIGHT-HOUR FLIGHT from Kuwait International Airport to Leipzig, Germany, was a blur. I took one of the sleeping pills the psychiatrist had prescribed to me at Bagram, which made me sleep most of the way.

During takeoff, I remember having a sense of disbelief that I was already on my way back home. In military travel time, it seemed record-breaking— as if I was wearing General stars. Someone later asked me if it was customary to get out so fast after having a sibling killed in action. I don't know if it's the standard operating procedure in cases like this. I am sure that my commander knew that I couldn't mentally stay in an active combat zone. He did his best to get me off of that mountain and on my way home. The exact timing of my departure came down to logistics and a little bit of luck. If the firefight we were in lasted much longer, helicopters wouldn't have landed in the middle of it to get me out. I may have had to wait until the next day, which could have thrown off all the conditions that allowed me to leave so fast.

The commander was correct that my head was not in the right place to do my job. At the time, I had no choice, so I muscled through until the helicopter landed. I didn't want to lose one of my guys because I was distracted. I didn't want my parents to get a second knock on the door because I couldn't handle the grief. I did what I needed to do to keep myself and my guys safe. I knew that I couldn't allow the intense, misdirected anger I was feeling to escalate.

I couldn't let the vision of myself running down the mountain, shooting everything that moved, become a reality. The other thoughts of how I needed to be there for my wife and son kept me from losing my mind and control. I also knew that lashing out would not bring Steven back.

I had a two-hour layover in Germany before departing for Atlanta. The layover was at the same airport where we drank beer and watched the Super Bowl a few months earlier. As much as I wanted to drink away the pain, we weren't allowed to drink this time.

There was a wall in the airport that travelers would put stickers on. Many of them were from their hometowns. Others were of unit patches that you might otherwise find on the shoulder of an Army uniform. I scanned the wall for any signs of Vermont soldiers passing through while waiting for the next flight. I found an oval "VT" sticker and another for a ski resort in Vermont. Another sticker reminded me of the black and white Jack Daniel's logo, which didn't help my desire to drink. I did take it as a sign that Steven wanted me to raise a glass for him at some point, though.

I knew it didn't matter whether he went through there or not. I searched for something - anything - to make me feel a connection to Steven at that airport. Despite traveling with over a hundred other soldiers, I never felt more alone.

I slept for most of the next flight, too, waving off the flight attendant when she asked me if I wanted a drink. The guy sitting next to me had to shake me awake when we finally landed in Atlanta.

Atlanta is one of the major hubs for military personnel returning from overseas. It is common to see military and military supporters in that airport. As we got off the plane, I noticed the groups of supporters there to greet the soldiers. I wasn't exactly feeling happy to be home at that moment. My brother just died, and I was engaged in combat less than two days earlier. I felt tremendous guilt for leaving Steven behind in Kuwait. The last thing I wanted was any pomp and circumstance over my arrival.

When we left Kuwait, we received instructions that we couldn't change into civilian clothes until we reached our final destination. That meant I couldn't change until I was back home in Connecticut. Despite those orders, I was very tempted to buy a change of clothes and ditch my uniform upon my arrival in Atlanta. I wanted to blend into the crowd, look like a civilian, and go unnoticed by the supporters. I still had my Army Combat Uniform (ACU) patterned bag, so I couldn't entirely avoid looking like a soldier. Even if I bought new clothes, I'd still stick out as a soldier with that bag. Instead, I ignored the supporters and looked at my ticket. I pretended that I was trying to figure out where my next gate was while walking past them. It was hard to take any pleasure in being welcomed home at a time like this. I missed being home and out of harm's way, but I didn't want to be home under those circumstances. Looking back now, I feel wrong about being rude to the supporters, especially since they gave up their free time to show their appreciation for people like me.

I don't know how different I would have felt had my return been with the rest of my unit a few months later. Situations like the one with the kid and the wooden gun didn't exactly make me proud of what I did over there either. That situation was the last thing on my mind at that moment, though.

I know that I didn't want to talk to anyone that day. A flight attendant on the final flight asked me why I was going home as I was boarding. I told her, "My brother had gotten killed in action." I also told her as nicely as I could that I needed to be left alone. She respected that. She even gave the couple sitting next to me a heads up about my situation before they got to their seats. They didn't say a word to me the entire flight.

When I landed in Connecticut, my parents, wife, son, Aunt Joanne and Uncle Phil waited for me at my gate. As we greeted each other, we all hugged and cried. The meeting in the airport terminal was the first time we all had an opportunity to grieve my brother's death together as a family.

My son, who was only nine months old at the time, was oblivious that we were all sad. He must have seen something that amused him and let out a loud laugh, which made us all laugh too. Even amid our grief, his laughter helped us remember that it was important to be grateful for what we had. I was thankful that I was finally able to see my son in person. For the last few months, I had only seen him in pictures Vicki sent me while I was in Afghanistan.

A State Police officer also met us at the gate. He escorted us out of the airport since many news crews were waiting to interview us. I couldn't figure out how the news crews knew we would be at the airport that day. Later, I found out that one of the local television stations called my parents' house to request an interview. My mom told them that they wouldn't be home as they were heading to the airport. She didn't have to say to them why they were going there. They were able to figure out that I was arriving home that day just from that brief conversation.

Loose lips sink ships.

Unfortunately, the crowds in Atlanta paled in comparison to what awaited me in Connecticut.

I told the officer that I needed to retrieve my rucksack from the baggage claim. He told us that the media was waiting to interview me near the baggage claim. Uncle Phil asked me what my bag looked like and went to grab it for me.

The Army rucksack looked like the same pattern as an Army uniform, plus mine had a DELUZIO name tape on it. I chuckled as I pointed to my uniform and said, "It looks exactly like this." It wasn't hard for my uncle to spot it out of the flood of black Samsonites rolling down the conveyor belt.

At this point, I still hadn't had an opportunity to change out of my uniform. So, random travelers stopped to shake my hand and thank me for my service as we walked out of the airport. I had whispered to my wife that I wasn't in the mood to be friendly enough to accept all the praise I was receiving. She picked our son up out of his stroller and handed him to me. Carrying my son let me "act" preoccupied, and it kept my hands busy so that I couldn't reach out for a handshake. It worked. No one else approached me on the way out of the airport.

We drove back to my parents' house, which was about half an hour away. The rest of my family – cousins, aunts, uncles, and friends were awaiting our return to their home. This short trip gave Vicki and me a little time to talk about my journey home before getting ambushed by everyone else.

As we turned into my parents' street, I could see vans from many local newspapers, radio, and TV stations. My initial thought was, "Fuck those people! Why can't they leave us alone?" I may have even said part of that out loud. I knew they were doing their jobs, but a lot of anger and hatred was welling up inside me.

During my time in Afghanistan, we were conditioned not to speak to the media if we ran into them. There were times that a nefarious reporter with an agenda twisted the words of a soldier in their story. We didn't want to be responsible for casting the war or the military in a bad light. Worse, we didn't want to set off an international incident based on some reporter twisting our words.

So, I turned to my mom and asked, "What do we do?" My mom and I didn't want to talk to the reporters at all. My dad did, though, which made me start to reconsider.

My parents both were grieving differently. My mom wanted to be left alone, sitting quietly by herself. She didn't want to talk to anyone at that point. On the other hand, my dad felt the need to be around people and talk about Steven almost from the moment they got the news about his death.

A major from the CT Army National Guard who was in charge of public relations met us in the driveway. He spoke up and said, "The media is going to run a story with or without your input. They will talk to people around town, a guy in a parking lot, or they could talk to someone who went to school with Steven. Regardless, they will run a story. Only you can give them the information that will let everyone know who Steven really was. Only you can do that."

After thinking about it that way, I realized he was right. I didn't want Steven's memory to die because I was too stubborn to talk to the media. His story wasn't one that I felt they would use to advance an agenda, so it seemed pretty safe to talk to them. My words wouldn't get twisted here. Lord help me if they did, though.

I switched gears and put my acquired feelings about the media aside. "Let's do it," I said. "Let's go answer their questions and tell them about Steven. I want people to be talking about Steven, and we need to be the one to start that conversation."

That week, I must have spoken to reporters from every newspaper, television, and radio station in Connecticut.

At one point, a local television reporter, Hallie Jackson, who happened to be close to Steven's age, came to my parent's door for an interview. My Aunt

Joanne let her in the house without asking who she was, assuming that she was one of Steven's friends. There were dozens of people coming and going all day long, so it was easy to make that mistake.

She hung out in my father's office until my aunt told us that someone was waiting for us there. I was appreciative that she stayed in my father's office. She could have taken advantage of the situation and spoken with all our family members. That helped me shake *some* of the "sleazeball reporter" vibe I had a few days earlier. I still didn't trust them all.

Besides the reporters, many friends and family members had gathered at my parent's house. They wanted to help however they could. They brought enough food to feed an army because I guess that's what people do in times like this. For a week or so, it was a constant flow of people and food.

It was hard not knowing a single person traveling with me during the two days I traveled home. So, it was comforting to be around people I cared about and who cared about me.

During that time, we all had a chance to reminisce about Steven and remember the good times we had with him. My parents had a home theater set up in their basement. We watched some old family videos of Steven being a goofball as a kid there. Others hung out around my parent's backyard pool. Then at night, we would turn on the local news to watch the interviews we had given earlier in the day. I still had a negative feeling about reporters, so I watched the news with skepticism. I anticipated that they would twist our words. To my surprise, all the reports were very respectful and didn't twist our words.

Through all this, I couldn't help but think that my brother was still back in Kuwait. I got home a few days before him, and it was difficult for me to leave him behind. Even at home, I kept making myself feel guilty for leaving him in Kuwait. "I will never leave a fallen comrade" kept echoing in my head. When I got on the plane to leave Kuwait, I felt like I was doing just that to my brother.

In reality, his body and every other casualty's body gets treated with the utmost care and respect. More importantly, he was never left alone.

The military investigated his protective gear in Kuwait. They wanted to determine if he was wearing it properly or even if he was wearing it at all. Unfortunately, no equipment issued by the military would have protected him where he got shot. The investigation concluded that his equipment was in working order. He had done everything he could have to keep himself safe before his death. While it was good to know that he didn't make any mistakes, it was little consolation in our grief.

Before returning to Connecticut, Steven's body traveled to Dover Air Force Base in Delaware. There the mortuary affairs team prepared his body for his return to us.

Upon arrival at Dover, he got taken into an EOD (explosive ordnance disposal) room. The EOD room has thick steel walls designed to withstand an explosion. The purpose of this room is to ensure that his body did not have any explosives with it that could harm anyone. A deceased soldier may still have a grenade, bullets, or other explosives in his or her possession even after being taken off the battlefield. The enemy could even booby-trap a body if they managed to get their hands on it. Since there are many ways that explosives could make it into the mortuary at Dover, it is safer for everyone to check all the bodies that come through.

After scanning his body for explosives, the mortuary affairs team took photographs of his remains and confirmed his identity.

Next, they performed an autopsy. The cause of death in his case was apparent - he got shot in the face. Even still, there is an autopsy done on every set of remains going through Dover. While the autopsies document causes of death, they are also used to help save lives. They can help inform recommendations to help prevent future deaths when they discover trends in the causes of death. These recommendations can lead to improved body armor, vehicles, and other equipment soldiers rely on to provide protection.

From there, the mortuary affairs staff prepared him for burial. The goal of the morticians is to make the body viewable for the family. Due to the violent nature of some military deaths, this isn't always possible. Even if a body is damaged so severely that it requires a closed casket, the morticians still prepare it impeccably. They prepare the body no differently than they would if it was suitable for an open casket ceremony. Everything from the uniform, the medals on their chest, and how they groom their hair gets done in precisely the same manner whether the body is suitable for viewing or not. I wanted to emphasize this because it shows how dedicated the mortuary affairs team is to the fallen. Even though no one will ever see their work in some cases, they do it to the best of their ability anyway. Their dedication is truly inspiring.

In Steven's case, his face and neck was the only area in need of reconstruction. They even covered up the scar on his forehead that I gave him when I hit him in the head with a baseball bat when we were kids. The rest of his body was, for the most part, in good shape. The morticians then cleaned his body and shaved him. Next, he was dressed in a Class A dress uniform, and then he was placed inside his wooden casket.

Later, our casualty assistance officers told us that they had the full autopsy report, including photos. They offered to show it all to us if we wanted them to. We asked them to just read the information to us. I suppose it didn't matter what the report said, though. It wouldn't have brought him back to us. When they inquired whether or not we wanted to look at the photos from the autopsy, my parents said "no." I asked if we could hang on to them for the future if we ever wanted to look at them. Still to this day, I've never seen those pictures.

While we waited for Steven's body to arrive in Connecticut, we began planning his funeral. It all felt surreal writing his obituary, meeting with the funeral director, picking out a casket, and finding a cemetery.

I did insist on having an open casket at his wake. The funeral director tried to discourage us from an open casket because he wasn't sure how the lighting would make Steven look in the church where we would have the wake. The lighting in a funeral home is better suited for an open casket wake, so he might not have looked great under the church's lights.

The morticians did do an excellent job patching him up, but he didn't look exactly how I remembered him. To me, it looked like he had a puffy cheek, almost like a baseball player with a wad of chewing tobacco in his mouth. My parents and I all vividly recall what his face looked like, except we recall it differently. They both remember seeing the wound near the bottom of his jawline while I remember it up near his cheek. Something like this is crystal clear in all of our minds to this day, but we still remember it differently. I think this shows how much the shock of seeing Steven lying in a casket affected us all.

Still, despite his appearance, I wanted an open casket so anyone who came to see him would recognize the sacrifice he made. I wanted everyone to know what happened to him, no matter how unpleasant it was to see. There isn't anything pleasant about war or the casualties it produces, and I wanted to make sure everyone who came to pay their respects understood that. In the end, we all agreed that it was best to have an open casket. It may have been unpleasant to see Steven with the puffy cheek, but it would let friends and family see him one last time.

My parents planned the procession from the airport to the funeral home in Glastonbury. When Steven's body arrived, we went out to the runway outside the Connecticut Air National Guard building. The Connecticut Air National Guard building was the same one I left from a year earlier for pre-deployment training in Indiana.

It was a hot and humid August day, and we had been standing out in the sun for a while, waiting for the plane to arrive with Steven. Our family waited along with an Army Honor Guard for the plane to come to a stop. As the doors opened and the casket carrying Steven's body emerged, my mother started to faint. Recognizing this, my cousin, Michael, and I grabbed her before she hit the ground. Someone ran off to get a chair for her to sit on. After a few minutes, the color came back to her face again. A combination of the heat and the emotion of seeing her youngest child carried off a plane in a casket may have caused her to become overwhelmed. It is also possible that she locked her knees, which has brought down even the strongest of people.

On the way home, we had a police escort for our convoy. The convoy consisted of the hearse with Steven's body and several other vehicles with friends and family members. I hadn't realized that the police would shut down about 25 miles on the Interstate for this trip. One car even got pulled over after trying to sneak through a barrier on an on-ramp. It was amazing to have the roads so empty of vehicles. Every bridge along the route had fire trucks parked on top of them. Firefighters from each town were there saluting, in Steven's honor, with American flags draped down the side of the bridges.

As a kind of farewell tour, we drove the route my parents planned on the way to the funeral home. The route took us past places that were meaningful to Steven. Sites such as our old childhood house, Leeza's family farm, the street where Steven proposed to Leeza, and our old high school. Lining the road to my parent's house were hundreds of small American flags placed in the grass by two of Steven's best friends. One of the last places we drove past was Ross Field, the Little League field in town. We saw players in their baseball uniforms carrying small American flags at various positions on the field. We learned that these boys were players on the last team Steven coached before he deployed to Afghanistan. They were the town champions that year, and these young players wanted to show their respect for their coach.

Lines of cars stopped as we passed by. The drivers got out of their cars and stood there with their hands over their hearts as we passed. Along the way, I also noticed many American Flags lowered to half-staff in his honor. It was nice to see how many people gave him that respect.

After Steven's body arrived at the funeral home, I realized Steven was never left alone. I had felt guilty about this in Afghanistan and Kuwait. The line, *I will never leave a fallen comrade* from the Soldier's Creed, echoed in my head as I saw the transfer case get loaded on a truck in Kuwait. I realize now that he was never left behind. Someone was always with him, and even in the funeral home, an honor guard got posted overnight so that he would never be left alone. It didn't resolve my guilt about leaving him behind, but it did make me feel better knowing that he was never left alone.

I will never forget the date of Steven's funeral because it fell on my wedding anniversary. It was only our second anniversary, and we would be spending it at my brother's funeral.

We had been at the wake the night before, where approximately 2,000 people came to pay their respects. Being in that receiving line was a test of endurance. We intended to spend about five hours at the church, but the church allowed us to have as much time as needed to accommodate everyone, many of whom we did not know. We ended up staying for at least six or seven hours, so we were pretty tired the next day. It was physically tiring to stand there all night, but it was even more emotionally exhausting. Regardless, I would have stayed there until the morning if people were still coming. There had been a long line to wait in, which they could have skipped to do other things. Instead, they remained in the heat to pay their respects. The Red Cross was also on hand to give water to people who came to stand in line since it was a warm summer day. Our family, friends, and the Family Readiness Group also brought us food and drinks.

We had the funeral at the largest Catholic Church in town instead of our family's usual church. When planning the funeral, the funeral director encouraged us to prepare for an enormous outpouring of support. Even with the large church, there was only standing room left for some of the later arrivals. With the available standing room at our church, we wouldn't have fit half as many people. The church we had the funeral at could fit at least 500 people seated and even more standing.

My cousin, Kevin, a cantor at his church, volunteered to prepare the entire funeral mass. He prepared the program and music choices and did a beautiful job singing during the mass. I don't know how he did it, but he did a fantastic job. After Steven's high school hockey coach delivered the eulogy, I got up to say a few words about Steven.

> *There are so many things to say about Steven. We'll be able to tell stories about Steven that will make us laugh until we can't catch our breath and cry until we run out of tears. He's touched so many lives in so many ways that every one of us could fill another lifetime with stories of the good times we've shared.*
>
> *Steven always lived life to the fullest. To paraphrase Top Gun, a movie we both watched about 100 times growing up, Steven "wouldn't be happy unless he was going Mach 2 with his hair on fire." He would always push himself to do the next bigger and better thing. He could ride a two-wheel bike before he was potty trained. He would throw himself in front of slap shots on the ice to defend his net, which he just*

as easily could have let pass by. Good enough just wasn't enough for him.

But he loved it all: the adventure and thrill of living life the Steven DeLuzio way. Unfortunately, since leaving for Afghanistan, Steven and I could not speak to each other by telephone. However, we were able to keep in contact through email. In his last email to me, he wrote about how he felt about his mission. Steven said: "We just got back today from three days camping out at the (Pakistani) border. Kind of funny to be using actual infantry stuff we learned in AIT. I loved it, the weather sucks at 10,000 feet, but I really dig the dismounted infantry stuff. It's more of a man-to-man fight. I got some great pictures of it, at least. Can't wait to share and see what you've been doing too." He went on to say: "Anyways, please keep all of this stuff away from anyone we may call a loved one. I, like you, try to keep the conversations happy when I call home. Anyway, stay safe, talk to you soon."

Steven died doing what he loved to do. Protecting those he loved most.

After the church service, we went to Holy Cross Cemetery in Glastonbury, CT, where Steven received full military honors. He received a 21-gun salute, a riderless horse, and a bugler playing taps. Many state, local, and federal politicians attended the funeral, and people from all military branches. There were 93 Patriot Guard Riders in attendance as well. All but about a half dozen of them were on motorcycles – the rest were in wheelchairs. The Patriot Guard Riders attend funerals of military and first responders when invited by family members. One of their roles is to protect mourners from harassment, which was a concern at the time with the Westboro Baptist Church (WBC) conducting protests at military funerals. The WBC has no affiliation with the Baptist Church. Instead, it is a hate group that would "Thank God for Dead Soldiers." Thanks to the Patriot Guard Riders, we never would have known if they showed up to Steven's funeral.

His funeral was a fitting and meaningful tribute.

Before the priest could say his concluding words, my father asked him to make an announcement. He wanted to invite everyone to a reception at the local country club. The priest looked around and said, "Are you sure? There are a lot of people here!" My father looked around and said, "Yes! Everyone can come!"

As soon as the priest concluded his remarks, people came up to our family to offer their condolences. A line was forming much as it had at the wake. After a short time, I started getting frustrated that people who hadn't taken the time to come to the wake the night before were lining up to offer their condolences. It seemed to me like it was inconvenient for them to wait in a long line at the wake, so instead, we had to wait out in the heat so that they could pay their respects. That was how I felt at the time, but in hindsight, I'm grateful that they took the time to honor Steven that day.

After the funeral, we headed to the country club for the reception. Of course, not everyone at the cemetery attended, but over 250 people joined us there. That reception turned out to be the start of more regular gatherings for years to come. For years after Steven's death, we held golf tournaments to honor and remember Steven and raise funds for scholarships and military charity donations made in his name.

7

Return To Civilian Life

AFTER MY RETURN HOME and Steven's funeral, I found myself struggling to get back into a routine. I didn't even pretend that I could get into a routine in the week between returning home and the funeral. Nothing about that week was even close to being normal. Planning your 25-year-old brother's funeral days after being in combat with no time to adjust is far from ordinary.

Even after that week, I found that the world I once knew a year earlier was much different from the one I found myself in after coming back home.

I had been a father for about nine months when I returned home. I hadn't spent any time around my son outside of a few days back home before deploying and a two-week leave in the spring. My wife sent me pictures and some videos of him crawling around while I was in Afghanistan. While those were great to have, they weren't enough for me to form a connection with him. At the time, I imagined most fathers created those connections pretty early on in their child's life. I wanted to make up for the time I lost with my son and my wife. It wasn't clear to me exactly how I should interact with either of them. The dynamic in our house had shifted, and I felt like I needed a lot of time to catch up.

A few weeks after Steven's funeral, someone from the Connecticut Army National Guard contacted me. As I would not be returning to combat in Afghanistan, I would need to travel to Camp Atterbury, Indiana, to process out of active duty. I don't know why I couldn't have processed out while in

Connecticut. At that time, the last thing I wanted was to be apart from my family. I even recalled how the Brigade Commander had convinced me to get home to my family instead of staying with Steven's body. I tried to push back and say that I didn't want to go to Indiana. I was still on active duty, and the Army owned me, so I didn't have a choice.

I received travel orders that would take me to Indiana for about three days to finish demobilization. I ended up traveling with a couple of officers who needed to travel to Camp Atterbury for other reasons. I don't know for sure what they were doing there - they may have told me, but I didn't care all that much at the time. They ended up staying at a hotel down the street from the base while I stayed in the barracks. I didn't see them much while I was there, which was fine with me. I wasn't in the mood for small talk with them. Since only a few soldiers were passing through at the time, I ended up getting almost the entire barracks building to myself.

The day after I arrived, I went into an administrative office. In the office, I got a checklist with everything I needed to do to get cleared off of active duty status. I needed to get physical, mental, and dental examinations. Then many different forms needed to get signed off by various offices scattered around the base.

All of this paperwork and exams were supposed to take me about three days to complete. I finished it in one. The officers who traveled with me seemed surprised that I got done so fast. I wasn't the nicest when I indicated that I wanted nothing to do with that place and wanted to return home to my family.

Yes, I rushed through the process and wasn't 100% honest in some of the examinations. Those forms were all that stood between my family and me. If the Army wanted accurate answers, I could have gone through this process closer to home.

My plan worked. Since I finished everything earlier than expected, I switched my flight to the following day. Getting back home a couple of days earlier than expected was an immense relief to me.

Now that I was home and no longer on active duty, I called my civilian boss to tell him that I could return to work earlier than expected. My boss, an Air Force veteran, said they weren't expecting me back until at least November.

That was when the rest of my unit was returning, and I was supposed to return. He told me he didn't need me to come back so soon. Because of his military background, he understood what I was going through. He knew that I needed some time to get my head straight after being in combat and losing my brother. I knew that jumping back into work wouldn't have gone all that well, so I took the next couple of months off.

The time after returning from Camp Atterbury to the time I started work again is a complete blur. I have little recollection of anything else that happened during that time. It didn't help that I wasn't sleeping much. Having an infant at home pretty much guarantees that you won't sleep through the night, although I wouldn't have anyway. I was also drinking much more than I should have. Sometimes the only way I'd get to sleep was if I passed out from drinking. I didn't recognize it as a problem at the time, but it was my way of numbing the pain I was going through. Drinking too much and sleeping too little contributed to how little I can remember from that time.

Several years ago, my family and I took a trip to Las Vegas. While walking around, I saw a sign promoting The Blue Man Group at a casino. I mentioned to my wife that I had always wanted to see them. She looked at me with a look of complete disbelief. She said, "We saw them back in Connecticut a little while after you got back from Afghanistan, don't you remember?" She even reminded me about some people we knew who we spoke to in the lobby. I can't remember any of it. I can't even remember my son's first birthday either. I know I was there for it because there are pictures of me at the party, but I can't remember anything about that day no matter how hard I try.

When I got back to work at my civilian job, I found it very difficult to drag myself out of bed and get to work. When I got to work, I would find myself sitting at my desk and staring off into space, completely unable to focus on my job. I worked in corporate finance at an insurance company at the time, and the work I did had no meaning to me anymore. It was boring, tedious, and it wasn't anywhere near as meaningful as fighting for your country. I also found it hard to relate to my co-workers anymore.

Meanwhile, my mom talked with me about how my dad was dealing with Steven's passing. She told me that his motivation for work had also been waning, and she wasn't sure how or if he'd keep working.

In Steven's high school yearbook, where it asks what you see yourself doing in the future, he put "taking over my dad's business." Because of that, my dad had envisioned Steven joining him in his consulting business. Steven could then take it over when the right time came.

Steven's desire to take over the business encouraged my dad to make this a reality for him. He would never be able to make this dream a reality now. My understanding was that my dad started finding less and less meaning in the work that he did. I began to think that if I joined him instead, he wouldn't lose the passion he'd always had for his work.

I didn't see any purpose in my work at the insurance company, so it couldn't hurt to help my dad out. I didn't know much about the work he did on a day-to-day basis, but I figured that I could find some meaning in working for him. In December 2010, I quit working at the insurance company, resigning only about a month after returning to work.

I began working at my dad's company as the "Director of Operations." The title was a fancy way of describing the administrative role that I had. At the time, I thought that the job would be a good fit for me. I received a tongue-in-cheek nickname of "Scotty Admin" while deployed. I always had a knack for taking care of administrative things, so I became the platoon's admin guy.

Even if this job with my dad wasn't right for me, I wanted to see my dad get his spark back. However, I soon became uncomfortable with being his full-time, salaried employee. I completed tasks quickly and wasn't sure what to do with the rest of my standard workdays. After about six months working for my dad, I realized that this job wasn't fulfilling either.

My dad's spark appeared to be back, and I felt like I was getting paid to sit around and do nothing most days. While this might seem like a dream job for some people, it wasn't for me. Looking back at that time in my life, I lacked the focus required to be the "self-starter" that the job required.

Later that summer, I sat down with my dad and told him that I thought it would be best if he found someone else to do this job. He got agitated and felt that I was leaving him high and dry. We ended up finding a compromise where I would switch to a part-time role. I would only work when he had administrative tasks that needed to get done.

Working part-time for my dad left me open to fill my days with other things. I started a business that got written up in Entrepreneur Magazine as one of the *100 Brilliant Companies to Watch*. It was exciting to get recognized this way, but I felt like a fraud at the same time. There was nothing brilliant about my company, and I didn't feel "brilliant." I couldn't even figure out how to get a whole night's sleep. "Brilliant" wasn't the word I'd use to describe myself at that time.

I realize now that I was struggling with some serious mental health issues at the time. And I dealt with them in a pretty unhealthy way. The only way I would get anything close to a whole night's sleep was to take sleeping pills or drink so much that I passed out. Sometimes I'd do both. Between sleeping too little and drinking too much, I wasn't doing myself any favors when it came to my work the next day. To make up for the lack of sleep or the hangover, I'd drink lots of coffee, which made it harder for me to sleep the next night. The cycle seemed like it would never end.

I also was cursed with some pretty unrealistic dreams that I desperately wanted to come true.

Early on after Steven died, I had a dream that he came to the front door and said, "I had to pretend that I died. I was on a secret mission where they had to fake my death. No one else can know about it, but I wanted to come to tell you. You can't say anything to anyone." When I woke up, I knew it was only a dream, but part of me thought, "Gosh! What if he is alive? What if I didn't have to be sad and could be even more proud of his dedication to the mission?" It all seemed like something out of a Hollywood movie.

I *knew* Steven had died, but it took me quite a while to even accept that it was real. At first, I was shocked and confused. My mind kept going over and over it as if there was something I could do or change to make him come back to us. There was a part of me that knew that was unrealistic. But the other part wanted to believe it was all a big mistake. It could have been someone else with the same name. Yes, at one point, I tried to convince myself there was another Steven DeLuzio who looked identical to him. I somehow tried to believe that this was all a case of mistaken identity.

Yes, I know how stupid it sounds.

From the day Steven died, I felt an overwhelming need to stay strong. I don't know how I did it, but I didn't even cry at the ramp ceremony where they loaded his body onto the airplane in Afghanistan. As I gave that salute in Kuwait, I badly wanted to break down but pushed that feeling deep down inside of me.

Looking back, I struggled with finding a sense of purpose and meaning in my life. Sure, I had a wife and a son at home, which was meaningful, but I needed more. I needed to fill the void of the sense of purpose I had while I was in Afghanistan.

Sitting around the house all day didn't exactly fill me with a sense of purpose. Without any long-term goals, I didn't have anything I could work towards to grow myself. I didn't have a sense of purpose that pushed me to achieve goals or pursue opportunities at this point. It felt like I was just coasting through life.

One way I tried to find a sense of purpose was by putting others before myself.

I was never left alone when I got the news Steven died through the time I got back home. The first evening after I learned about Steven's death, I had someone escort me to the Chow Hall on the base. I didn't realize it at the time, but I was on suicide watch, so I wasn't going to get left alone. I wasn't hungry but figured I should eat since someone had taken the time to go with me. I hadn't had anything to drink for a few hours at that point, and it was hot, so I did feel dehydrated. I got two cups of water. I wanted to drink both cups but felt awkward because the person who escorted me had nothing to eat or drink. So, I pretended like I had brought her water and passed a cup to her. It was a small start of me doing things for others even when they weren't in my self-interest.

When I was back in Connecticut, one of the ways I tried to be helpful was to create a memorial website for Steven. I had been designing websites since I was in college, so it was easy enough to do. When I was in college, my dad was starting his business, and I asked him if I could help with anything as he got started. He said, "Yea, make me a website." At the time, I didn't know how to do that, so he told me to "Buy some books and figure it out." So, I did. Little did I know I would be using those skills to build a memorial website for my brother years later.

I used the website I created for Steven to share pictures, videos, and stories with family and friends. The website later became the site for his memorial fund, SGTStevenDeLuzio.com. This fund raises money for other military charities and scholarships.

While building this website was a way for me to keep busy, I was also doing it so that others could look at photos, videos, and remember Steven. Other's grief was what drove me to put that website together.

My general attitude was that if there were something I was capable of doing, I'd do it. I didn't want my parents to have to deal with things like handling Steven's estate. Which, to be honest, is something I never thought I would have to worry about either.

Since I didn't think any parent should worry about their child's estate, I volunteered to take it on. I had no idea what I was getting into, and it was very taxing to figure it all out. I had to go to probate court to file all the paperwork and get Steven's estate in order. I did it all wrong about a half-dozen times and had to keep going back to get it straightened out. I now know that I should have hired a lawyer to do this. It's tough to think with a clear head when you are in the depths of grief.

Even though some aspects of my coping were normal and healthy, I tended to keep everything inside. Maybe volunteering to help with things like the memorial website and Steven's estate were a distraction for me, so I didn't have to deal with my emotions. Those distractions may have helped others, but they kept me from healthily processing my grief.

Then my anger and unresolved feelings would manifest in inappropriate ways.

I put my feelings aside on that mountaintop when we started taking fire from the Taliban in the village. That was necessary so that I'd be able to survive to see another day. Pushing my feelings aside was fine temporarily, but I couldn't keep doing it forever. **Eventually, if you keep sweeping things under a rug, you'll end up with a floor you can't walk on.** Pushing all of my feelings under the rug was what I ended up doing.

It was about five months before I even realized there was a problem with my mental state. At that time, I could see that I had a lot of displaced anger. Whenever I got upset, I'd unleash my rage on other people rather than dealing with it healthily.

My short temper would often coincide with everyday, minor events. When my son would cry, I'd try to soothe him. If I couldn't console him and get him to stop crying, I'd get over-the-top frustrated. I would think, "I'm not a good father if I can't fix this," and would get angry at the situation. Other times, I'd make a simple mistake, like dropping something or taking the wrong turn while driving, and I'd start yelling about it. I wasn't the most pleasant person to be around at this time in my life.

Vicki was taking note of how quick I was to anger too.

The final straw was when our dog, Roxy, threw up on our white carpet in our bedroom. As I watched it happen, I completely lost it. Roxy was standing right at the edge of our tiled bathroom floor when she threw up. It would have been so much easier to clean up if she had thrown up in there. I got so mad and started screaming at her. I yelled that she had missed the tile by a few inches, and now I would have to rent a steam cleaner to clean it up. Like a dog would understand all that.

I realized I wasn't acting like myself. My behavior wasn't reflecting who I was, or at least not who I wanted to be. I sat down on the floor next to Roxy, who seemed to forgive me for losing my temper right away by snuggling up next to me. That was little consolation, though. I knew in my heart that something needed to change.

Vicki approached me shortly after and said that this wasn't how things were going to go. She knew I needed help and said I should talk to someone. I nodded in agreement with tears in my eyes over the realization of the person I had become.

I was not getting better at controlling my misplaced anger, and these outbursts were happening almost daily. After discussing it with Vicki, we agreed that it wasn't like me to behave this way. I'm the guy who helps people, not hurts them. At least, that's who I wanted to be.

Around this time in early 2011, I went to the VA to have my knee evaluated. It was still bothering me after falling from the helicopter. The doctor I saw did a very brief exam and said that "I'd be fine if I stayed off of it for a few weeks. Take some Advil if the pain got worse."

At this point, it had been about four months since the fall, so I couldn't imagine what a few more weeks of rest would do for it. So, I decided to get a second opinion. I had private insurance through my job, so I went to a civilian doctor. He determined almost immediately that I needed to have surgery to fix my knee.

I had next to no faith in the VA doctors who first examined me. Even though the VA would not pay for procedures done outside the VA, I chose to have the surgery through the civilian doctor. The VA will pay for some exams outside of the VA now, but that was not the case in 2011.

After the surgery, I faced months of physical therapy and recovery. My doctor told me that it wouldn't be until November of that year that I would recover enough to return to duty for training. Since I was still a member of the National Guard unit I deployed with, I still had to attend training one weekend per month and two weeks per year. I couldn't walk without crutches for a few months. Being on crutches meant that I couldn't participate in any training with my unit. When I attended the training, I ended up sitting there watching everyone else train. I felt useless.

Given my physical and mental state, I started looking into how I could get discharged early. My contract with the Army National Guard would end on November 8, 2011, unless I decided to re-enlist. If I didn't re-enlist, I would be in an Inactive Ready Reserve (IRR) status for another two years. As a result, I could get called up for active duty and sent to another unit within those two years. Staying in the Army meant that I could deploy again. I didn't think that another deployment was something that my family or I would be able to handle.

If I waited until November, I feared that the discharge wouldn't get approved, and I would get placed in the IRR. I needed to see if there was any possibility of separating early.

Honorably discharging someone before their time in service ended was uncommon but not unheard of either. Most other situations that I knew of wouldn't get classified as an honorable discharge. Since I had served honorably, I knew I didn't want to get discharged under any other status, no matter how much I wanted to leave the Army.

I came across a section in the Army Regulations titled *Surviving Sons and Daughters*. It said, "Any son or daughter in a family whose parent or one or more sons or daughters served in the Armed Forces of the United States and (1) was killed in action. (2) Died as a result of wounds, accidents, or disease while serving in the US Armed Forces. (3) Is in a captured or missing-in-action status. (4) Is permanently 100 percent disabled...." Commanders are to approve requests for the separation of soldiers who meet the above criteria.

Surviving Sons and Daughters sounded like it was referring to me. Before bringing this to my chain of command, I went to talk with Chaplain Nutt. Chaplain Nutt knew our family's situation pretty well, and I knew I could ask for his advice in confidence. What he told me was that it had to be my decision. But, regardless of what I decided, the Army would support me in my decision.

So in April of 2011, I drafted a letter that requested an early discharge under the *Surviving Sons and Daughters* section of the Army Regulations. I handed it directly to my Platoon Sergeant, who I knew well from our time in Afghanistan. I bypassed my Squad Leader, who was the next above me in the chain of command. He had recently replaced the Squad Leader I had in Afghanistan. I didn't trust that he would understand my situation or my desire to separate from the Army. I even doubted that he would pass my letter up the chain of command.

After waiting for a few weeks, I received a letter in June of 2011 that told me I successfully separated from the Army. Being honorably discharged meant that there was no possibility of a future deployment for me. I had an enormous weight lifted off my shoulders. There was also a tremendous feeling that I had lost a part of my identity. One morning I woke up still a soldier, and by the time I went to sleep that night, I was a civilian.

There was very little closure or a transition period for me. I had not considered this abrupt transition when I requested the discharge. The only thing I had left to do with the Army was to turn in any equipment that I still had. There were no formal goodbyes to the guys I had served with in Afghanistan. One month I was at training with my unit. The following month, I wasn't.

This transition is common amongst military veterans, but it might make more sense for civilians to think of it like when someone retires from their career. When someone introduces themselves, they might say they're a doctor, mailman, teacher, chef, etc. After they retire, though, what are they? They've lost the identity that they held for so many years. It's very similar with veterans. Even though I was only a soldier for a short time, it was a label I wore with pride. Then all of a sudden, that label abruptly changed to "veteran." It was still an honorable label, but it was an adjustment to get used to nonetheless.

8

Family Life

I WAS VERY FORTUNATE to have had my family's support in moving forward with my life. While I wanted better for myself, I was also motivated to be a good husband, father, and son. I knew making the changes I needed to make wasn't going to be easy, but that it would be worth it.

The last thing I wanted was to end up divorced or alienated from my family because I didn't take the time to readjust. I know many military families have been ripped apart by stressful events. To avoid getting to a breaking point, I decided to do whatever I had to do to become a better version of myself. I knew communication was going to be essential for me.

Vicki and I decided to get married soon after we started dating. She became pregnant only about six months after we got married. Since we are the type of people with a "shit or get off the pot" attitude, we both realized that I needed help right away. The path I was on was destructive, and I wouldn't figure it out without some help.

Vicki and I have always loved each other and been on the same page about most major life decisions. Being on the same page makes marriage so much easier than if we were to argue all the time. Yet, the core of our relationship has been our open and honest communication.

The level of communication we've enjoyed has allowed our trust and mutual respect to grow. Vicki and I have been married since 2008, and we've always communicated well. Even early on in our relationship, we made communication a priority. Very often, we will even know what the other is thinking from a look or hand gesture. Communicating was, of course, difficult to do while deployed.

One of the lessons that I learned is that communication is one of the most significant assets to have in the military. If your radio goes down or you are out of range of other soldiers, you get cut off from the outside world. In that scenario, you can't call for a medivac or air support. You can't learn new intelligence, such as enemy movement towards your position. Lives depend on good communication on the battlefield.

Communication with your spouse is just as important. Many fights couples face could be avoided if everyone in the relationship is on the same page. I'm not saying that you always will agree with the other person, but try to understand their point of view.

While I was in Afghanistan, we knew we had to keep up our regular communication to avoid this problem.

It was a blessing that the Army allowed me to bring my cell phone with me to Afghanistan. Anticipating the considerable cost of international calls while on a soldier's salary, I wasn't planning on using it. But I looked into my plan's coverage to see what my options were.

It turned out that I was right about the expense of international calls. Still, I found out that I had a package that included unlimited international text messages. When I asked Vicki if she was okay with communicating by text messages, she said, "Absolutely!" In our minds, it was better to communicate often by text than only once in a while by phone. Plus, text messaging didn't need both of us to be awake at the same time. Given the time difference between Afghanistan and the East Coast, it wouldn't be very often. Communicating by text message allowed us to be in touch with each other much more often.

So for the duration of my deployment, we had entire conversations over text messages. It worked very well for us. So well, that to this day, we have continued to prefer texting over calling whenever we are apart.

After I got home, I came to appreciate how well Vicki and I communicated even more. Vicki was a great support system for me during a difficult time in my life. I can only imagine how difficult it would have been if we hadn't been able to have open conversations with each other. She is generally a very positive yet realistic person. She helped me see the upside of bad situations and gave it to me straight when she noticed that I was heading down the wrong path. Of course, we've encountered the kinds of challenges that are common with couples. The ability to communicate helped us overcome those challenges and make ourselves stronger.

I know that it couldn't have been easy for Vicki to witness how my deployment and Steven's death affected me. She was very good at dealing with bad situations when she needed to. Still, she did not focus much on what was happening in Afghanistan or the rest of the world. When I was in Afghanistan, Vicki kept busy and didn't let herself sit around at home for too long. She knew that if she did, she would end up worrying about what was going on in Afghanistan. She avoided watching the news or reading newspapers since she knew it would make her nervous. Those things would take her focus away from her primary job, taking care of our son. From her perspective, there wasn't much she could do for me while I was on the other side of the world anyway. It didn't do her much good to dwell on what was going on over there.

She kept busy by throwing herself into being *the* parent, which was a role she maintained even after I came home. After returning, I did ease myself into taking on a parenting role. But Vicki took on more than her share early on after I returned home. She didn't expect much from me since she knew I had so much to process.

She had developed systems for caring for our son, Adam, which worked well for her when I was away. Sometimes it seemed to throw everything off course if I got in the way of the process. Like any other kid, our son didn't come with a handbook, so she had to figure out how to meet his needs on her own. She had done a great job at it, and I was playing catch up when I came back home. Having a baby to care for when Steven died wasn't the easiest thing in the world. But he gave us both the chance to latch on to something bigger than ourselves. He gave us light to cling to during a very dark time in our lives.

Over the years, I found that serving something bigger than yourself is helpful when facing a loss. From the day that Steven died, my family was that thing I would serve.

After my commander told me that Steven died, he asked if I was going to be okay. He recognized that I could hurt myself with the weapons I was carrying. I remember thinking to myself that I couldn't do something like that. I wasn't suicidal. I had a wife and a child at home. No matter how much the pain of losing my brother hurt, how could I leave them behind? What about my parents? Could I let them lose both of their sons in one day? And if I did, what would that help anyway? Easing my pain wouldn't make their pain any better. A child I barely knew would grow up without a father. A wife I loved would become a single mother and struggle to raise our son on her own. Grieving parents who would be dealing with the loss of one son would have twice the amount of grief. No, I couldn't do that to them. They were my mission.

Even if I didn't have to grieve Steven's death, Vicki said she would have done things the same way after getting home. She would have acted as a mentor to me, rather than handing the baby off to me and taking a "mommy vacation."

She said this because I still would have had a grieving process of sorts to go through. By that, I mean grieving the change in lifestyle from being on alert 24/7 in a combat zone to returning to civilian life. That is a crucial thing for any spouse to recognize in their service member who returns home. There will always be a transition period. Expecting a service member to jump back into a "normal" routine once they are home doesn't mean that they are mentally ready to do so. While deployed, we operate at a very high-intensity level. It is much different from taking care of a child. It was wise of Vicki to realize that taking it one step at a time and not rushing into things was what I needed.

Adam was almost nine months old when I came back, and now as this book gets released, he's twelve years old. As time went on, I learned a lot about parenting from Vicki, and Adam has grown to be a curious, intellectual kid. We can't keep enough books in the house to feed his intellectual appetite. He gets through them all so fast because he's interested in learning about the world around him.

About a year and a half after I returned from Afghanistan, we had Charlotte. Charlotte is now nine years old and has a bubbly cheery personality. She is very often dancing or doing cartwheels around our house. We had Raymond about fourteen months after Charlotte was born. Raymond, who is now eight, is energetic and can be sort of a goofball at times.

Each of my kids has their own unique personality. Learning what works and does not work for them has kept us on our toes. Vicki is good at noticing what motivates them, so I've tried to follow her lead.

Before Raymond was born, when we only had two kids, Vicki and I would often each take care of one at a time. Usually, I'd look after Adam since Vicki had more experience with babies. After Adam, I didn't experience much new baby stuff, so I experienced it all for the first time with Charlotte. It was like being a first-time parent to me all over again when Charlotte was born.

Vicki and I agreed when we first got married that we only wanted to have two children if we were able to. At that time, we thought Steven would marry his long-time girlfriend, Leeza, and that they'd have kids. We imagined our kids growing up together, as Steven and I had done with our cousins. It turns out that Steven and Leeza had been dating for almost eight years when he died on August 22, 2010. They had planned to be married on September 17, 2011.

I had grown up in a big family with lots of cousins. After Steven died, we realized that our kids would never have that experience. We decided to have a third child to make our own family bigger. We wanted our kids always to have someone to play with at home. And as they got older, we wanted them to have someone they could count on to be there for them.

When Raymond was born, we soon realized that having three kids was a huge difference from having two. One of us would *always* have to watch more than one kid at a time. A few days after Raymond was born, Charlotte got into some diaper rash cream and got it all over her face and mouth. Since our hands were full with the other two kids, we weren't paying close enough attention to what she was doing. We weren't sure what was in it, so we called poison control. We were relieved to learn the brand we were using had no harmful ingredients. That incident made it clear to us that parenting three children is drastically different from parenting two children.

A few months after Raymond was born, we decided to move from Connecticut to Arizona. We had been talking about moving for a while but never acted on it. We dealt with a lot of bad weather, including Hurricane Sandy and massive winter storms. Back then, we would complain about the weather and the high cost of living in Connecticut.

Most people understand not wanting to pay a lot in taxes and longing for a warmer climate. While it was true that we didn't like the weather or the taxes in Connecticut, they were inconveniences we could have looked past. They were easy scapegoats for why we wanted to move.

After returning from Afghanistan, it seemed like everyone knew who I was. After having my face on every local television station and newspaper, people started to recognize me. If you're looking for fame, this isn't a bad thing. The feelings I had in the Atlanta airport about the pomp and circumstance hadn't changed much at that time. I was feeling the strain of being "the brother of the soldier who got killed." Add that feeling to all the attention our family was getting, and I felt like I was in hell.

In March of 2011, I was in a Dunkin Donuts buying a coffee. A well-meaning guy approached me and offered to buy me the coffee because he recognized me from the news. I know it was from a good place in his heart, but I felt disgusted that he would give me a gift of any kind. He was only doing it because he knew about my brother.

Gifts, in my mind anyway, tend to have a happy or at least a positive connotation. You get gifts during happy times or a celebration. This time was a time in my life that was anything but happy. I accepted the coffee from him so that I wouldn't be rude, but I never drank it. It made me sick to my stomach thinking about drinking it. My birthday was also a few days away at the time, and it soured receiving birthday gifts for me altogether. Receiving gifts, or even when friends and family wish me a "happy birthday," still makes me depressed to this day. My birthday was never something I celebrated much before, but now I avoid celebrating it altogether.

Even the physical therapist I saw after my knee surgery knew who I was before I even walked through the door. I remember during the first appointment I had, I explained how I got the injury. It came up that I came home early because my brother was KIA in Afghanistan. She seemed almost to cut me off as she said she already knew all that.

I felt trapped. In my mind, I only had two options. The first was to be a hermit and never leave my house (which I had considered at one point). The second was to move away from Connecticut altogether.

My wife and I had considered moving to another town in Connecticut, but I didn't think that would have helped. There were many Gold Star family events all over the state, which I felt pressured to attend anytime one came up. Being in large crowds was, and still is, an anxiety-producing nightmare for me. Despite the good intentions of the organizers, I never liked attending those events. If I moved away from Connecticut, I would have an excuse for not going to them.

It seemed like the best thing for us at that point was to get away from everything and start over in a new place.

I told my parents that we would be moving to Arizona in a few months, and they didn't receive our news well at all. It wasn't only my parents who weren't happy about the news. Most of our family and friends weren't particularly happy about our decision either. But we needed to make the difficult decision to create some space to be off on our own. I needed to get away from all the things that were keeping me down. So, we packed up our things and drove off to the other side of the country.

We left Connecticut on New Year's Day 2014 and took about six days to drive to our new home in Arizona. With two cars, three children four years old and under, plus a dog, I'd say we made it pretty fast.

Even though we moved across the country, I want to acknowledge that our family was, and still is, important to us. And we didn't move to get away from family.

Each of our kids' names comes from a family member in one way or another. We thought about using Steven for Raymond's first name since he was born after Steven's death. But we didn't want him to grow up feeling like he had such big shoes to fill with that name. So, we gave him Steven as a middle name instead. His first name, Raymond, was after my brother's favorite NHL hockey player, Ray Bourque.

Almost three years after we moved to Arizona, my parents moved out here too. They did not want to watch Adam, Charlotte, and Raymond grow up over Facebook.

We got a clue that they were considering moving before they told us. On one visit out to Arizona, my parents announced they were going for a drive. My parents don't usually take drives for the sake of it. Especially not on a trip where they came to visit us and see their grandkids. They weren't going sightseeing either - we're about four hours away from the Grand Canyon, and there's a whole lot of nothing in between our house and there. There is usually a destination or purpose motivating them to get in the car and go someplace.

I said to Vicki, "How much do you want to bet that they are looking at houses?" My mom had later told me about her desire to move here after my dad retired. She had also concluded that he was not going to stop working anytime soon, if ever. She figured that they may as well make a move while the grandkids were still young. Vicki, at the time, was a real estate agent, so she was happy to be able to show them around Arizona to find their new home.

For several years now, we've enjoyed regular Sunday dinners with my parents. We go to their house, and our kids swim in their backyard pool or play games in their home. I think our time apart made us appreciate what we have today.

I'm not sure if I'd be writing about how my story evolved into a happy one if Vicki and I had remained in Connecticut. Having a change in environment was a big help to my emotional state. The period where Vicki and I were in Arizona, away from all the attention, helped make us stronger.

Planning has always been a staple of Vicki's personality. She always had a plan A, B, and even a plan C for those "just in case" situations. Vicki learned from my deployment that you can't always count on your plans. That you might have to adapt to the situation as it unfolds. She might have planned to talk to me at a particular time while I was in Afghanistan, but oops, some jerk-off decided to shoot up our base so that I couldn't call home.

I learned that no matter how well you plan a mission, you'll end up improvising when shit hits the fan. As the saying goes, "a plan never survives the first contact with the enemy."

This mindset helped our family become more resilient when dealing with the many sudden changes we faced.

Vicki or I couldn't have planned for when she started having seizures for the first time. She had been battling a cold, which didn't seem like that big of a deal. Then out of nowhere, she started acting strange. I decided to take her to the hospital to get her checked out. Shortly after arriving, she started experiencing grand mal seizures. No amount of planning would have prepared us for that.

Vicki ended up hospitalized for two weeks, part of which she was in a medically induced coma.

After she came home, she had *a lot* of work to do in her recovery. The seizures had impaired her speech and brain functionality. She used to be very active, and in the months following, she had trouble even walking normally. She wasn't allowed to drive either for at least three months after her last seizure. She had continued having seizures at home for about eight months. None of which required hospitalization, but they were scary nonetheless. It wasn't until almost a year after her first seizure that she was able to drive again.

When Vicki couldn't drive, she relied on me, her parents, friends, and Uber to get her around. I took on the "family chauffeur" role, which became pretty taxing on me while running a business.

Early in her recovery, Vicki had many doctors' appointments, so I spent a lot of time away from work. Being away from the office wasn't easy for me, but we made it work by adjusting the times I would work. I still managed to keep my business operating while helping Vicki in her recovery.

Vicki has made many adjustments to support my career, and this time I had to step up more to help her out. I know I don't tell her this enough, but I'm grateful for her faith in me when I chose to start a business. Vicki understands how much thought I put into big decisions, such as becoming an entrepreneur. She knows me well enough to see that I've weighed all the pros and cons and will make the best decision for our family.

She'd also rather have me happy with the work that I do than be miserable with it. Even if it meant making more money, she'd rather have me happy and fulfilled with the work I do.

Finding purpose in my work and feeling passionate about it makes me a better husband and father.

9

Mental Health

EARLIER I TALKED ABOUT HOW MY WIFE and others, including me, noticed that I wasn't acting like myself anymore. Before my deployment and Steven's death, I was a kind, caring, and pretty level-headed individual. Afterward, I became an angry person who had a very short fuse, drank too much, and slept too little. I was a train wreck at first. And since I was busy making sure everyone else was okay, I didn't even notice it.

At the time, I couldn't see how these things were affecting my life. I couldn't see how any individual outburst affected my family or how my lack of sleep and drinking affected my ability to do my job. I couldn't know how each crappy decision I made compounded on top of all the others. And what's worse, I would think about my outbursts and justify them by blaming others for what they did. It never occurred to me that I should look at myself to figure out what I was doing wrong.

I would spend all night lying in bed, trying to fall asleep. At some point in the early morning hours, I would give up, usually around the time when the baby woke up. After I changed a diaper and put the baby back to sleep, I'd brush off the lack of sleep and figured I was up for the day. I'd tell myself that I could get through the rest of the day with an extra cup of coffee or an energy drink. I was right for a while because I would be able to get through that day without too much trouble. I got used to running on very little sleep when I was in Afghanistan. We would often work long shifts throughout the night.

Coffee and energy drinks kept me going throughout my shifts.

The next day would be a repeat of the day before. With little sleep and a caffeine lifeline, I'd only have a *slightly* harder time getting through the day. It wasn't a problem that a little more caffeine couldn't fix. It became an endless cycle where the "cure" made the situation worse than it was initially.

I stopped running and exercising after I returned home due to my knee injury. It was embarrassing how out of shape I became. I could have continued exercising by lifting weights but hated doing that. I still do.

One drill weekend, someone commented, "It looks like you've bulked up. Are you working out?" "Nope, I'm getting fat," I thought to myself.

I found that physical activity helped to keep me grounded while I was training to go to Afghanistan. It was a great outlet while we were over there too. After returning, I stopped caring about what I was eating and did nothing for exercise.

Our base had a small gym with a few treadmills and weights. I'd often go there to work out before or after a shift or whenever I had some downtime. Working out was especially important when posted to base security. You might find yourself sitting around for hours at a time in a guard tower with no outlet for exercise. At least when you're out on patrols, you are walking around and carrying heavy body armor and other equipment.

I'm sure that the lack of exercise after returning from Afghanistan took its toll on my mental state.

It wasn't until the day I pushed my dog that I realized I needed to get help. I remember sitting on the floor thinking to myself, "What the fuck did I do? What kind of monster have I become?" Vicki came in to talk to me, and I may have surprised her when I told her that I agreed I had let this go on for too long.

It took an event so far from who I was to make me realize that I wasn't acting like myself. That was my "rock bottom" moment. I am thankful that I didn't let it go any farther than that. I would never have wanted to injure someone or say something that I wouldn't be able to take back. This rock bottom moment was when I first got a hint that only I was in control of my actions.

I knew I needed to seek help with how I felt and start taking care of my well-being. I decided to begin counseling shortly after the incident where I pushed my dog across the room. I knew I would never be over losing Steven, but I had to learn how to handle some of the complex feelings I had avoided.

In February 2012, I started going to the Vet Center. The Vet Center provides readjustment counseling services and is part of the VA. It's open to any service member who served on active duty in any combat theater or area of hostility. It's also available to family members of those killed in action or during their service. I checked a few of the boxes that made me eligible to be able to use their services.

When I first called the Vet Center, I was pretty nervous and didn't know what to expect. They told me that everything I said would be confidential, but how confidential was it? Would I get sent to some mental hospital if I said the wrong thing?

It turns out that my worries were for nothing. I immediately felt a tiny bit better after I made that first call to schedule an appointment. It wasn't that the person doing the scheduling had said anything particularly profound to me. Instead, it was the fact that I knew I wouldn't have to carry this burden around by myself anymore. There was going to be someone there to help me through it.

The first appointment was a "getting to know you" type of appointment. The appointment allowed the counselor to get an understanding of what I was going through. It also allowed me to get a feel for whether the counselor was a good fit for me. As we got to know each other, he assured me that everything we talked about would stay inside that room. No one else would know what conversations took place in that room.

I continued seeing my counselor at the Vet Center for almost two years. I found a huge benefit in being able to talk to someone who listened without judgment.

I don't want to give the impression that my wife wasn't helpful to talk with because she was. It's just that some of the things I needed to be open about were kind of embarrassing to admit. I felt like I didn't want to put the weight of everything I was carrying on her. I felt more confident talking about what I had going on because I knew what I said wouldn't leave the room. The confidence allowed me to get clarity on some of the issues I was trying to resolve.

We talked about how the anger I was carrying started right after I shot my last shot in Afghanistan. I remember feeling anger at the Afghan army welling up inside me during that day's attack. I was so pissed that they couldn't secure their own country and that we had to be there at all.

I was angry at our interpreters for the same reason. Don't get me wrong, our "terps," as we called them, were great for the most part. But after learning about Steven's death, I wished they had done more to secure their own country. I resented the fact that we had to come and fight their war for them. I was angry at all the people in the village that we had patrolled through earlier that day. I was mad at every single Afghan – whether I had ever met them or not.

I downright *hated* the people of Afghanistan. Only about an hour after learning of Steven's death, my sadness and grief turned into pure anger.

The treatment I received at the Vet Center got me to a more stable place mentally. I wasn't perfect, but I stopped relying on sleeping pills and alcohol, which seemed like a win. I could sleep through the night at least a few days a week, which was another win. Generally, I felt like I was in a better place mentally than I was before.

After moving to Arizona, I stopped going to counseling for a few years. While I still dealt with some anger issues from time to time, I felt like I was in control most of the time.

In late 2019 I started feeling a change in my mental state. I had started a business around the time we moved to Arizona, and for years I enjoyed the work that I was doing. However, now it was beginning to feel like a drag.

When I noticed the change in my mental state, I would sit down to work and get distracted. I would often spend an entire day staring off into space. It was much like what I experienced at my insurance job after returning from Afghanistan.

It wasn't only my work that I noticed was suffering. It was difficult for me to find enjoyment in *anything* that I once found to be enjoyable. For some reason, I thought it was typical not to want to do some of the things I previously enjoyed doing.

I used to love playing golf before my deployment. I would look for any excuse to play at least a few times per month during the warmer months when I lived in Connecticut. Whether it was with friends or relatives, I would always look forward to going out to spend a few hours golfing. I even have pictures of me teeing up a ball in Afghanistan. Someone had donated some clubs and balls to the Morale, Welfare, and Recreation center (MWR) on our base, so we'd crank shots into the mountain. Now that I live in Arizona, I could play golf year-round if I want. I've only played a couple of times at work conferences in the years I've lived here. I didn't even particularly enjoy it, though. For a while, I blamed it on having young kids at home and that it was hard to get away for an afternoon. The truth, though, is that I had no desire to play.

Since my son was born a short time before I deployed to Afghanistan, I had no idea what it was like to be a father before leaving. When I got home, I didn't recognize it to be odd that I struggled to enjoy doing things with my kids.

A father's heart should fill with joy when he plays with his kids or watches them laugh and be silly. Yet, I often found myself coming up with excuses to avoid doing those things. Sometimes I don't have the energy to do *anything,* let alone chasing after energetic kids. Other times I worry that bad things will happen after doing something fun with them. As if any good that I experience has to be offset by something terrible. I know this doesn't make a lot of sense. There isn't much logic behind these thoughts. But I convinced myself that bad things would follow the good times and happy moments. Avoiding these fun and happy times, in my mind anyway, is a way to prevent bad things from happening.

I had once enjoyed going to concerts and sporting events. I convinced myself that it was normal to avoid large crowds. Now I feel like I'm on edge and need to get away any time I'm anywhere near a crowd or even small groups of people.

I reached out to the VA again to seek mental health counseling. Their evaluation found that I had chronic PTSD and a major depressive disorder. Unfortunately, none of this was new. I had been living with these conditions for years. I never realized it, though, until now. I had been convincing myself that I was fine, all while not understanding the toll it was taking on my life.

I would go places and do things with my family, but it would be rare for me to come up with the plans. I didn't even care if I participated in family activities. I never had the drive to come up with things to do on my own, either. It always seemed like I was just along for the ride as a passenger in someone else's life.

When I did take part in these family activities, I rarely was present in the moment. I rarely enjoyed any of it. I would never be comfortable whenever I would go out, and I'd want to get back home where I was safe.

At home, my mind would wander too. It wouldn't be easy for me to be present in the moment. I would feel like I had little to no energy in either situation and couldn't focus on what I was doing.

I even found myself having issues with my memory. Whenever I have to pick up more than one or two items from the store, my wife and I joke that I'm in "list territory." If you send me to the store to get six things, I'll come back with, at best, two of those things if I don't have them all written down. Sometimes I even forget when it's only one thing I need to pick up. I may even be staring right at the thing I am supposed to get, and my mind will draw a blank.

At first, it seemed funny, like my "old age" is showing. But now, I realize the traumatic experiences I lived through have significantly impacted my mind.

PTSD can cause memories to be hazy or to be missing altogether. It can jumble timelines, so you don't remember what order events happened. It can also make it challenging to learn new information.

After realizing how significant the impact has been on my memory, it isn't amusing anymore. On the other hand, there are some things I would like to forget but can't seem to get out of my head.

Sometimes it feels like I am standing in Afghanistan with my weapon aimed at the kid on the back of the jingle truck.

I can feel the pressure of the butt of my weapon pulled into my shoulder. I can feel the smoothness of the stock as it rests against my cheek. The cold metal of the charging handle is resting on my nose. I see the orange arrow from the sight on my rifle. It's aimed a little to the child's left, as my training taught me to do when "leading" a moving target. I can feel the pressure on my thumb as I move my safety from "safe" to "fire." I hear the click it makes when it snaps into place. I start to feel the pressure on my index finger as I place it on the trigger and start to squeeze. My heart starts racing when I think about ending this kid's life.

The feelings turn to confusion again when I realize the gun that the kid is holding isn't a gun at all. It's nothing more than a piece of wood shaped like a gun. I lower my weapon and feel the pressure of the butt of my weapon fade from my shoulder, cheek, and nose. I can feel the safety switch back to the "safe" position as the sling picks up the slack of the weapon on my shoulder. I realize that I almost shot a kid who didn't deserve to die. I can feel the pressure in my chest and the coolness of my breath as it passes through my lips. "Fuck", I say out loud to no one in particular as the gravity of the situation becomes clear to me all over again.

Memories like that get replayed in my head over and over again. It would be wonderful to forget those memories altogether, like how I've forgotten many of the good times I've experienced since returning home.

Instead, I end up staring off into space, replaying those moments in my mind. "Replaying" isn't even the right word for it. It's more like I'm reliving them because it feels like I'm still there.

If you were to close your eyes and think about that scenario, you might be able to convince yourself you're there too. The feelings are real, and I don't need any convincing that I'm there. For a few moments, I'm no longer sitting on my couch in the living room. I'm standing on the hot, dusty pavement only a few yards away from the Pakistani border in Eastern Afghanistan.

I also realize that my willingness to shoot a young child also means that I was able to do my job. I was willing to protect my soldiers at any cost, even if it meant doing something terrible like killing a child. I understand that I didn't get tunnel vision and miss that the kid was only holding a piece of wood. I was able to see the situation unfold before me and make the best decision possible, which ultimately saved his life and possibly kept me out of prison.

I know that I did a good job, but the haunting memories persist in my head.

Traumatic events affect your mind and your memory strangely. I would categorize Vicki's hospitalization for seizures as traumatic. At the time, I didn't know what was happening to her or if she would ever recover. The doctor asked me if she was taking any medications or had any allergies, and my mind went blank. It would have been easy for me to rattle off her allergies and medications a few hours earlier. The stress from this traumatic event made me forget all that critical information. I guess the stress made me so focused on keeping her alive that I couldn't think of anything else.

Since I was diagnosed with PTSD and depression, I am getting treatment through the VA. I'll continue with it until I can manage it independently since I don't know if my feelings will ever go away for good. Through therapy, I hope to learn how to manage my emotions better than I had been for the last ten years.

10

Looking Forward

THIS BOOK HAS TAKEN ME YEARS TO WRITE. After I returned from Afghanistan, I began writing down important events that occurred. I knew that after time your memory starts to fade. While some of those memories were difficult to think about, I didn't want to forget them either.

I remember my dad talking about how he wished he knew more about his father's time in the Navy during WWII. I figured that someday my kids and grandkids would want to know about my time in the Army. So, I wrote down as much as I could remember without a plan for what to do with it. I was only trying to document those events for future reference.

So, a lot of the information in this book got documented back then.

Yet, these were only notes – not in any organized format and not polished at all. It wasn't until May 2019 that I decided that I wanted to write this book.

My parents and I got invited to The White House by President Trump for a Gold Star Family event. The event took place shortly after Memorial Day 2019 in honor of 50 families who lost a loved one to war.

The initial invitation came via a phone call to my dad from The White House. They asked if we would be able to attend. When he told me about the phone call, I thought it was a scam. I even suggested to my parents that they ignore it, fearing that they might get taken advantage of if it were a scam. However, it turns out that my dad had sent a letter and a copy of a book that he wrote to President Trump. The caller from The White House referenced this letter and his book in the phone call, so they had a good feeling that the call was legit. A few days later, we received a formal written invitation in the mail from The White House, which made it real.

The night before the Gold Star Family event, we had managed to schedule a private tour of the West Wing. Most tourists do not get to tour the West Wing unless they know someone who works at The White House.

I was scheduled to get into Washington DC that afternoon, which would give me plenty of time to get to the hotel, drop off my bags, and head over to The White House. As our flight approached Washington, the pilot told us that we couldn't land due to the weather. We also didn't have enough fuel to wait out the approaching storm, so we would have to land in Norfolk, VA, to refuel.

On the tarmac in Norfolk, there were at least a dozen other planes that I could see, who never pulled up to a gate. I presume they were waiting to refuel while in the same predicament as we were. With the growing number of planes on the ground, we were uncertain of exactly when we would be able to take off again.

The flight from Norfolk to Washington is less than an hour, so I still had enough time to make it to The White House if the plane left soon. But if we were there for more than an hour or so, I didn't think I would make it.

I had considered figuring out how to get off the plane, find a rental car, and drive the rest of the way. But I knew the traffic around Washington is terrible, so that would have taken me even longer.

It turns out that the plane only stayed in Norfolk for about a half-hour. Enough time to refuel and get back in the air. I made it to Washington later than expected, but I still made it. And I had enough time to get to my hotel, drop off my bags, and change before the tour.

The tour of the West Wing was pretty incredible. We toured the Oval Office, Roosevelt Room, Cabinet Room, White House Mess, Rose Garden, Press Briefing Room, and Situation Room. Well, the Situation Room was off-limits to us. But someone opened the door as we were passing by, so I was able to see a few clocks inside the door - nothing more, I promise! The clocks I saw displayed the time in various international cities with the city name printed underneath. One had "POTUS" printed underneath it. I'm assuming that the clock gets updated with the local time wherever the President is. When we got to the Press Briefing Room, we sat in the chairs where the news reporters sit. My parents and I pretended to ask questions as if we were talking to the Press Secretary, which was pretty fun. That was also the only room we could take pictures in since it's on television every day. I wish I could take photos of the rest of the West Wing because it was incredible to see.

The next day my parents and I toured the monuments around Washington. We also made a stop at Arlington National Cemetery. After becoming a Gold Star Family, we have had the opportunity to get to know many other Gold Star Families. Several of them have loved ones buried at Arlington National Cemetery, so we went to pay our respects.

The last time I was at Arlington was during a family vacation as a kid. During that trip, Steven tried to stomp out the eternal flame on JFK's grave. Although it is a solemn place, we had a good laugh when I asked my parents if we should check if the flame is still burning!

Later that night, we returned to The White House. There we waited outside the gates with dozens of other Gold Star family members to get escorted into The White House by the Secret Service. After checking our IDs, they sent us through the most intense security screening process I've ever seen. I guess if you're going to be meeting the President, they don't want to take any chances with security.

After the screening, it seemed like The White House staff was expecting royalty to arrive. The Marine Corps Band was playing in the Entrance Hall. High-ranking military and government officials spoke to us with genuine interest. Deputy Secretary of Defense, David Norquist, sat down with my parents and me and asked us about Steven. Not only did he ask questions, but it was also apparent that he cared about what we had to say. It was nice to see that these high-ranking officials took time out of their day to show respect to these Gold Star Families.

We were allowed to explore much of the East Wing on our own. The amount of history contained in some of those rooms was remarkable. We got to see many historical paintings, sculptures, and even some items that former Presidents once owned. Some even dated back to George Washington.

Later that evening, we were asked to get in line to wait our turn to have our pictures taken with President Trump and First Lady Melania Trump in the Blue Room. I usually don't get too star-struck when I've met famous people in the past. They're just people, right? But this was the President of the United States. The man who has the nuclear launch codes took time out of his day to spend with us. I remember walking in and not knowing what to say other than, "Hello, Mr. President, it's a pleasure to meet you." I didn't give what I'd say much thought before we entered the room. As we walked into the room, he didn't wait for us to approach him in the center of the room where he was standing. Instead, he walked over to my mom and hugged her. As we followed President Trump back to the center of the room where our pictures would get taken, he pointed up above and said to my parents, "Steven is looking down on you right now." The First Lady, Melania Trump, was equally gracious and told us that she was "sorry for your loss."

I had brought a challenge coin we had made in memory of Steven and planned to present it to President Trump. The traditional way to give a challenge coin to someone is by palming it and passing it in a handshake. When we entered the Blue Room, a naval officer told us not to have anything in our hands as we greeted the President. Of course, I didn't listen and palmed the challenge coin in my pocket. As I approached President Trump, I popped the coin into his hand with a firm handshake. Receiving the coin caught him off guard, but he still thanked me for it. After handing over the coin, I peeked over my shoulder to see if any Secret Service agents were going to tackle me. Luckily, I got one past them!

The President had a challenge coin rack on the table behind him when he appeared on television from the Oval Office. I only hope that Steven's challenge coin made it to this rack.

After we had our photo taken, we went into the East Room for the memorial celebration. There, the President, Vice President, and other officials joined us in honoring the sacrifices of our fallen loved ones.

During the ceremony, I reflected on how important this day was in my life. After all, it isn't every day that you get invited to The White House to meet the President. As I was thinking about this, I realized that the only reason we were there was because of Steven's sacrifice. It was a sobering reminder of why we were there.

After leaving The White House, I mentioned to my parents that I wanted to turn those old notes I made after returning from Afghanistan into a book. Something about that event sparked a flame in me and made me want to make something out of those old notes. So, with the encouragement and support of my parents and my wife, I began writing this book.

I started writing the book around the same time that I started my podcast, Drive On Podcast. My idea for the podcast came from realizing how many veterans struggle after serving. I learned that far too many go without getting the help they need, and sadly some even take their own lives. My podcast interviews veterans about the issues they've developed as a result of their service. Some have dealt with homelessness or abused drugs or alcohol to cope with their problems. Others survived suicide attempts, broken marriages, and more.

While those messages may sound depressing, I share them to give hope to the listeners. Every one of those guests I mentioned struggled after leaving the military. But there was a light at the end of the tunnel for each of them. They figured out how to grow from their experiences and become better people in the process. My goal is that my listeners will see that there is hope for them too. Selfishly, it serves as a reminder that there's hope for me as well.

Not every story I share on the podcast is a happy story, but they all have a positive message to share. One of the veterans I interviewed, Wes Black, was one of Steven's best friends. He was the first to reach Steven after he got shot. On the podcast, Wes spoke frankly about the burn pits in Afghanistan and their effects on his body.

Wes was diagnosed with stage four colon cancer after returning from Afghanistan. His cancer became linked to the toxic chemicals he got exposed to from the burn pits on his base.

There's no sugar coating that. It sucks. Even with such devastating news, Wes was still determined to live his life without letting the possibility of death drag him down. Despite being exhausted from chemotherapy treatments, he would still get on the floor and play with his son. Or, they would chase each other around the yard. In his words, he said: "Granted, in my weeks of chemotherapy, I'm not feeling great, but how do you tell a three-year-old that we can't go to the park today? Like, 'daddy doesn't feel good.' You know, you can't do it, you have to stand up, you have to be a man, you have to be a father." He even continued to work as a firefighter during some of his chemotherapy treatments.

In addition to fighting for his life, he fights for other veterans as a spokesperson on the burn pit issue. National news networks and other publications have interviewed Wes to help bring awareness to the hazards we all faced with the burn pits in Iraq and Afghanistan. Any service members who served on a base with a burn pit should sign up for the VA's burn pit registry. The registry will help the VA track cases to the bases that individuals were assigned to see trends in sicknesses that develop over time. Hopefully, this will lead to better recognition of the hazard that burn pits create.

Many of the guests I talk to on the podcast have discovered alternative therapies that work for them. There are physical activities like mountain climbing, endurance races, and yoga. There are arts like music, painting, and photography for those who want something less physically demanding. I have even discussed forms of therapy involving animals like equine-assisted therapy.

I found that these individuals are the types who are not afraid to improvise, adapt, and overcome. The VA may have recommended medication or talk therapy, which may not work for everyone. These veterans have found other means of treatment that are effective for them.

One such guest on the podcast was Edward Santos, a soldier who served with me in Afghanistan. When he returned from Afghanistan, he began going to PTSD therapy groups at the VA. At one of those meetings, the counselor told him that a Vietnam veteran taught other combat veterans how to paint like Bob Ross. Since Santos grew up watching Bob Ross paint "happy little trees" as a kid, he figured he would give it a try. It turns out that the first painting class he took changed his outlook on life. In his words: "The art brightened up the world for me when I would sit there and paint. It taught me that the more I put my art into place, the easier it became for me to come out of my shell and speak to people. I was more of a hermit after coming back. Always putting myself down, that I failed, that I didn't become a super-soldier. I wanted to be, but my body didn't allow me to. And every time I would step backward, I'd get into painting, and it would just draw me out as this different person."

A few months after interviewing Santos on the podcast, I decided to give art a try. I bought a sketchbook and some pencils since those were things I was comfortable with using. I didn't want to jump into painting as he did. I hadn't painted anything since I was a kid during art classes in school, and I wasn't even all that good at it back then. I didn't want to get discouraged by painting like I was in 3rd grade all over again. All I wanted was to be able to sit down and sketch out something or someone. I didn't want to take a class to figure out all the different paints, brushes, and other supplies you need. It's supposed to be fun.

When I first started sketching, I didn't know where to begin. I started with a couple of cartoon characters and other things like that. Something that didn't need to be so precise and would still come out looking decent. These first few sketches let me build up some confidence with my artwork. Later on, I started sketching the faces of actual people, which are some of the hardest things to draw. Since then, I've drawn my wife and kids, brother, and grandfather in his Navy uniform. I've also sketched things and places that were significant to me at the time.

I found myself taking pride in the fact that my sketches were resembling the subjects I was drawing. When I am working on these sketches, I get *very* focused on what I'm doing. I don't realize it while I'm drawing, but I focus a lot on all the details on the paper. None of the other worries in the world seem to be able to enter my head.

After getting more comfortable with my artistic side, I also decided to give painting a try. I found that I enjoy that too. Painting takes more time and is harder to put down than sketching is. But I see a lot of the same benefits regardless of the medium.

The most significant benefit I have found is that I stop thinking about the memories that I'd rather forget. I don't have visions of the Afghan kid I almost killed while I'm painting. I don't see the soldiers carrying my brother's transfer case as it gets loaded onto the plane at Bagram. I also don't overthink about the dangers in the world.

Usually, I throw on my headphones, listen to some music, and get lost in the moment. Most importantly, my mood seems to improve while I'm drawing or painting. That improved mood often tends to carry on throughout the day after I've finished.

One day after painting with my kids, my wife noticed that I seemed happier while painting together. It was true, I was. I enjoyed taking an idea and turning it into something beautiful on the canvas. Then I saw how much fun my kids had while creating something great, which made me even happier.

It was a strange feeling for me to be happy. It's not that I've never felt that way before. After returning from Afghanistan, I seemed to forget how to find enjoyment, even in things that previously made me happy.

When I got back from Afghanistan, I would describe my emotions when I wasn't angry as just "numb." I never got super excited about the happy or fun things I'd experience. It's almost as if I didn't care about them happening at all. That's not to say that I wouldn't put on a fake smile and pretend to be happy every once in a while. I knew my family needed some happiness. I didn't seem to be able to feel it on the inside, though.

I need to realize that I can create happiness, even while suffering from PTSD and depression. The hard part for me is forcing myself to do the things that make happiness. And at the same time, reducing some of the other negative feelings that I experience. Sometimes I need to force myself to seek out pleasure, which isn't always easy to do.

As I wrote about earlier, I often find myself completely lacking any energy or motivation. On some days, anything more than getting out of bed, eating breakfast, and taking a shower is a struggle for me. Some days I sit in my home office and feel like I don't accomplish anything because I struggle to focus on anything meaningful. When I find myself feeling this way, I try to muster up the energy and motivation to pull out the sketchbook or paintbrushes. If I can spend a little time creating some artwork, I usually feel a little better.

While all this helps, I still know that my mental health still needs work. I continue to get therapy at the VA to help me overcome some of these issues. If I were to continue living life as I had been since I returned from Afghanistan, I couldn't expect to get any better. I have to try to do better for my family's sake, and that's what I'm doing.

With this book and my podcast, I want other veterans to know that they're not alone. While the podcast intends to help others, I've found that it also has helped me by speaking with the guests I've had on the show. None of the stories that I share on the podcast will be the same as yours or mine. However, I hope the guests' experiences will leave their mark on the listeners of my podcast.

I want readers of this book and listeners of my podcast to know that it is not my intention to be judgmental with either of them. I want readers and listeners to understand that I'm not going to judge you for suffering from PTSD. It's a pretty natural reaction to have when someone experiences a traumatic event. As I've demonstrated in this book, I know what it's like to find yourself drinking too much, avoiding people or places, getting angry, and not wanting to get help. My goal for being so raw and open about what I've experienced is that hopefully, you'll understand that these are just symptoms of the condition from which you or a loved one is suffering. PTSD might have distorted your perception of reality. The reactions you are experiencing might be completely normal, given the situation.

I want you to know that there is hope for you. Before you pick up the gun or the pills, know that what you're experiencing may not be an accurate depiction of reality. With help, you can gain clarity and begin to see the world for what it is instead of through the lens of PTSD.

We don't hesitate to go to the doctor to get a cast when we break a bone or get chemotherapy when we have cancer. No one questions you for staying home from work when you have the flu. There isn't a stigma around taking care of your physical health.

Yet, there tends to be a stigma around taking care of your mental health. Some people view getting mental health treatment as being "weak," or they need to just man up and deal with it. Imagine telling a cancer patient to quit whining about their cancer or telling someone who just broke their leg to suck it up and get back to walking without crutches. Ridiculous, right?

Why should mental health be treated any differently? PTSD and other mental health disorders can be debilitating. If we want our loved ones to operate at their full potential, we should be encouraging them to seek the help they need instead of bashing them for it. If you're looking for someone to support your decision to seek help, you've found him right here. I'm in your corner rooting for you!

Through my podcast, I've been fortunate enough to interview dozens of veterans. Most of these veterans are strangers to me when we start recording. I start each episode by asking the guests to tell me about themselves. Even when talking to a stranger, breaking the ice like this is pretty easy for most people to do. Once we get talking, the conversation usually flows very well.

What I've discovered is that there is a strong connection that many veterans have with each other. We would share this connection even if we didn't serve together. By the time I've finished an interview with another veteran, we're talking with each other as if we were old friends. I don't know if it's in the way we speak or think, but something unites us.

My conversations with veterans have made me realize a few things veterans commonly struggle with when they get out of the military. One is a sense of purpose, and the other is a sense of belonging or camaraderie.

I experienced this myself when I first got back from Afghanistan. The civilian job I was working on seemed petty and meaningless to me. I struggled to relate with my co-workers, and they seemed to struggle with connecting with me. I felt isolated, as if I were the only one in the world who ever experienced this. More importantly, I didn't feel like I had anyone to turn to who would understand what I was experiencing.

I discovered that I had to find a new sense of purpose. I had to find something bigger than myself. For me, being a number cruncher at an insurance company wasn't going to cut it. It took me a while, but I found a sense of purpose in hosting my podcast. It allows me to serve the veteran community and those who are struggling in silence. It lets me show them that they're not alone and that there is hope for them.

It has also allowed me to talk with some incredible individuals I likely wouldn't have spoken to otherwise. Hearing their stories and perspectives, like those I wrote about earlier, has been inspirational.

These conversations have allowed me to open up and talk about some of the things I went through. In a way, podcasting has been therapeutic for me too. It also has opened my eyes to the fact that *everybody* has a story, and they're all worth telling. It doesn't matter if a veteran has not deployed or seen combat. Their story is just as worthy of being shared.

All of those stories have unique perspectives, which are only known to the individual who experienced it. Even two people who experience the same situation will perceive it differently. I wrote earlier about events during my basic training, which I attended with about 50 other soldiers. I bet if you asked each of them to recall various memories of that time, you'd get 50 different sets of memories. It's not that any of them were wrong or remembered incorrectly. It's just that certain events will stand out to each person a little differently. Even during the Afghanistan deployment, I'm sure that only a handful of the guys in my platoon would remember when I almost shot that kid or the old man. But there probably are some other events that stand out to them that I won't recall at all.

When I read the sworn statements made by soldiers in Steven's platoon about his final mission, all the reports differed to some extent. They were all a part of the same mission, fighting against the same enemy. However, as any good infantryman will tell you, they were spread out over a wide area as they should be. Naturally, their stories will differ a little. It's not that any of them are incorrect, though. Each soldier on that mission was in a different position looking at the enemy from different angles and witnessing events from different perspectives. Some engaged the enemy, while others gave aid to the wounded or even carried out the deceased. The people they spoke to and the things they saw varied from one individual to the next.

That's why everyone needs to tell their story. Without a wide range of perspectives, it's not easy to get a complete picture of what took place. It wasn't until I read all 21 sworn statements that I could get a clear enough picture of what had happened that day to write about it in this book.

I want all Americans – current service members, veterans, and civilians – to understand what the war in Afghanistan was like for our troops. Stories like the one you've read in this book will help put the pieces together so that you can get a better understanding of what it was like to deploy to a combat zone. I encourage you to read other stories told by any of the thousands of other service members who served in the Global War on Terror. Some saw more combat than I did, and others didn't see any at all. They all have a story to tell that is part of the bigger overall picture of the war.

The stories of those who didn't see combat are no less valid than those of veterans who did. Sometimes I'll talk to a veteran who didn't deploy or deployed and didn't see any combat. They'll tell me that they feel like their service wasn't significant enough. Like they didn't do anything meaningful if they didn't put their life in harm's way. They might even feel silly about experiencing PTSD symptoms.

I'll tell those veterans that knowing something terrible *could* happen can be enough to cause a mental health problem. Feeling like you have to "keep your head on a swivel" can make you hyper-vigilant and filled with anxiety.

While deployed, this hyper-vigilant behavior might have seemed normal and even desired. After all, we want to make sure we identify any potential threats before they can hurt us. The problem comes when we fail to turn off this hyper-vigilance when we get home.

Cars that cut you off on the highway, or trash that blows across the street, are usually not concerns at home. Yet, when we forget how to turn off our constant state of alertness, we wind up experiencing symptoms of PTSD.

The behavior of returning combat veterans is something that many Americans don't understand. Even the somewhat mundane "war stories" deserve to be told. Most Americans would not learn these lessons unless they experienced them first-hand.

When I was in Afghanistan, one of our interpreters asked why I wanted to be there. I told him that I never wanted my kids' generation to have to come there with a rifle and body armor as I did. I'd gladly fight a war so that they wouldn't have to experience it first-hand.

But I want them to learn about the sacrifices that so many service members have made at home and abroad so that we can be free. I want them to appreciate all the good things we often take for granted here in America, much like my dad did when he took us to Tijuana as kids.

Afterword

The war in Afghanistan drew to a close in a strikingly similar fashion as the Vietnam War. At the time of this writing, the Taliban has re-taken control of the country and sent the elected president, Ashraf Ghani, fleeing the country.

This exit has left thousands of Afghans and Americans stranded inside the country. While the United States and other countries are sending flights into Afghanistan to evacuate those left behind, it may not be enough to save all of them.

Understandably, many Americans, Afghan war veterans especially, are feeling like this war was a wasted effort. Many have grown frustrated by the war's outcome, especially with how quickly the Taliban regained control.

I don't feel like this war was a wasted effort. Steven's death and the thousands of other deaths were not a waste of life. Instead, I think that every single service member who took part in the war did what was needed to keep Americans safe at home.

In the nearly 20 years since we entered the war in Afghanistan, zero airplanes have crashed into an American building in a 9/11 style attack. That is because we took the fight to the enemy's home turf. They were so busy fighting us there that they didn't have the opportunity to plan another attack in the United States.

I count that as a victory.

Not only that, though, but coalition forces also helped build schools for the children to get an education. Many of those children are adults now, and they know the benefits of the education they received as a child. Hopefully, as they become parents, they'll want the same, if not better, for their children.

There are villages in Afghanistan that got running water, electricity, and other infrastructure for the first time, sometime during the last 20 years.

The Afghans in those villages now know the benefits of the infrastructure we provided them.

Education and modern conveniences that we take for granted here in the United States might be enough that the Afghans are willing to stand up and fight to keep. If not that, then it might be worth fighting for the relative peace that many Afghans enjoyed while we patrolled their streets. The terror they will inevitably live with during the Taliban rule will not be as palatable.

In 1968, my grandmother on my mom's side was diagnosed with cancer. She went through chemotherapy, which was a painful and terrible process to endure. But she beat it. She and the doctors fought to wipe out her cancer, and she went into remission. Unfortunately, her cancer returned 20 years later, and she ended up succumbing to it in 1989.

Were her doctor's efforts back in 1968 made in vain? I don't think so. I was born in 1982, and without the chemotherapy, I never would have known her. She lived long enough to meet most of her grandchildren. I was only seven when she died, but I have memories of her that will last a lifetime.

The Taliban is Afghanistan's cancer, the coalition troops are the doctors, and the patients are the people of Afghanistan. The patient and the doctors fought hard against it, but it was not for nothing.

I hope that all coalition troops can find a positive angle to view this war. Instead of dwelling on the lives lost in combat, focus on the lives saved back home by not allowing a repeat of 9/11. Don't worry about the equipment handed over to the Taliban, instead think about the freedoms that Afghans enjoyed while we were there. The gift of freedom is priceless, even if the recipients only experienced it for a short time.

We did what our country asked us to do. Be proud of that.

Pictures

I wanted to include some pictures of places and events that I discussed in the book. The photographs may help add some context to the story. The following section contains photos and a brief description of the image.

Picture 1 – This photo is of Steven, me, and some of our cousins at Westover Air Reserve Base. Steven (L) and I (R) are wearing white hats.

Picture 2 - It was almost impossible for Steven not to make a goofy face whenever a camera was around. There are dozens of photos of him with a goofy face or photobombing someone's picture.

Picture 3 - These photos are from the "Turning Blue" ceremonies, which took place the day before both of our graduations. Steven asked me to present it to him, which was a big honor to me. I was happy to have Steven present me with mine too, but I was ecstatic that he was home from Iraq and safe. The Infantry Blue Cord is to be worn by qualified infantrymen assigned to an infantry unit. It is presented for the first time to new infantrymen at a Turning Blue ceremony. This ceremony signifies that they have completed all of the training requirements required of infantrymen.

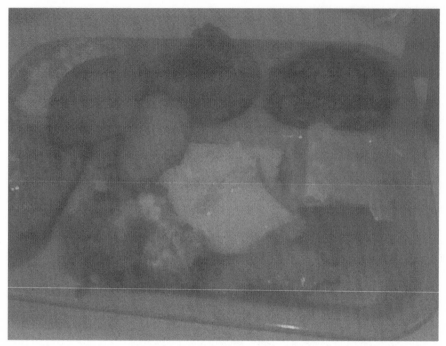

Picture 4 - Thanksgiving 2009. This photo shows what our Thanksgiving dinner looked like that year. We were on a range at Camp Atterbury, IN, when called to eat. A Congressman was serving soldiers, so I'm assuming we got pulled off the range to eat to be there for the photo-op. The food tasted about as good as it looks. At least it was warm.

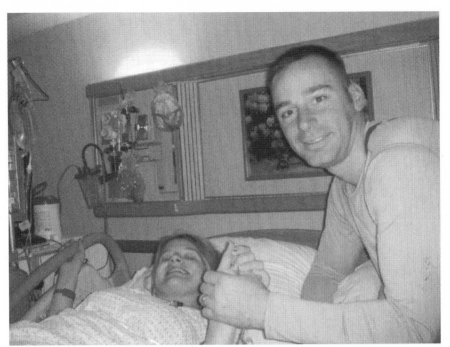

Picture 5 – November 28, 2009, started with me waking up at Camp Atterbury, IN, to a typical training day. Later that day, I would be racing to the airport to catch a flight home for the birth of my first child. I made it with a little over an hour to spare shortly after midnight the following day.

Picture 6 - (L-R) This picture shows Leeza, Steven, Me, and Vicki at our son Adam's christening during the Christmas leave before deploying to Afghanistan.

Picture 7 – This photo is the last I have with Steven and me in it. It was taken at the airport a short time before we boarded our flight back to Indiana after Christmas to resume training. The last time my parents saw Steven alive was shortly after taking this photo.

Picture 8 – This photo is of one of the Humvees that got stuck in the mud while we were driving on some off-road trails after several rainy days at Ft. Polk. It took us about 18 hours to get all of our vehicles back to the motor pool, even though we were only a few miles away. Even though it was a long and miserable night attempting to free these vehicles, I feel like the experience brought our platoon closer together.

Picture 9 – We were allowed two beers each during our layover in Germany while heading to Afghanistan. We landed in Germany on Super Bowl Sunday just in time to watch the game. This photo shows the first of many beer stops in the shop at the airport. Two beers.

Picture 10 – This photo shows me on top of the mountain that surrounded a portion of FOB Torkham a few days after arriving at the base. You can see there was very little other than dirt and rocks surrounding the FOB. The loose dirt created incredible dust storms that would make it impossible to see more than a few feet in front of you during the summer.

Picture 11 – The burn pit we had on FOB Torkham is pictured here. It was on the mountain that surrounded part of the FOB where many of us worked when assigned to base security. Other times the wind would blow the smoke down the hill towards our living quarters. Burn pits like this have been linked to various health issues in veterans and have been called our generation's "agent orange." Agent Orange refers to the toxic chemicals that troops in Vietnam were exposed to and suffered health issues from after returning home.

Picture 12 - This "jingle truck" is similar to the one that a kid popped up from and pointed a wooden toy rifle at our guys. We had offloaded all the cargo from this one because a bomb-sniffing dog detected explosives on the truck. I learned to use the explosive residue testing kit before deploying, so I tested random samples of the cargo, the cabin area of the truck, and various other points. If any residue were present, it would show up on the test. Fortunately, it was a false alarm, and the truck did not contain any explosives.

Picture 13 – When a car gets stolen in the US, it often gets sent to Mexico. From there, it gets shipped to Pakistan or other countries. The vehicles eventually make their way to Afghanistan with American (and Canadian) license plates still attached. We started confiscating the license plates we came across and ended up with almost 100 license plates. Ripping the license plates off vehicles didn't make the Afghan drivers happy, who viewed the American license plates as a status symbol. I sent a list of the license plate numbers to law enforcement in the US, which helped bring closure to many vehicle theft victims.

Picture 14 - Afghan children often live in extreme poverty. They would visit us near the border, asking for empty water bottles we had so they could sell the plastic. One time we gave them full bottles on a hot day so they could drink them. They dumped the water and packed the empty bottle in their bag. Kids like this got mad at us for closing down the road when we searched the jingle truck for explosives pictured earlier. Even though they might get blown up, they wanted to pass by to get to school.

Picture 15 - This photo is of an outdoor bazaar that would be set up on our base periodically. Local Afghan vendors would bring many things to sell, including clothing and knock-off sunglasses, and jewelry. One of the things they sold that soldiers loved were cheap bootleg movies. You never knew what kind of quality you'd get when you bought one, but for $5, it was worth a gamble.

Picture 16 – "Welcome to Pakistan Khyber Rifles." The Khyber Rifles are a paramilitary group, which is part of the Pakistani Army's Frontier Corps. This location's role is to assist local law enforcement with border patrol and anti-smuggling operations along the Khyber Pass. The Khyber Rifles have a history that dates back to British colonial days. The Pakistani soldiers we encountered at the border were never very friendly towards Americans.

Picture 17 - A view of all the trucks backed up miles away from the Pakistani border when Pakistan would shut down the border. Hundreds of trucks would get backed up in the wadi (a dry riverbed) outside our FOB.

Picture 18 - I don't remember which base this was on, but it is one of the many fast-food restaurants I came across. There were McDonald's, Subway, Burger King, and others. All the most refined dining for folks who were going to be fighting a war.

Picture 19 - The MWR on FOB Torkham had golf clubs and golf balls we used from time to time. Golf tees wouldn't go into the rock-solid ground, so we improvised with a spent round from the on-base shooting range.

Picture 20 – During my mid-deployment leave, I got two weeks to come back home. The time flew by, but it was great to spend some time with my family without worrying about the dangers we faced in Afghanistan.

Picture 21 - This photo is of a typical Afghan house we encountered. Homes like this are made from a mixture of mud and straw to create bricks you see on the right side of the picture. The roofs are flat and built with mud and straw placed on top of wood poles. More than one family may live in a house like this, and it isn't uncommon for 10-15 or even more people to live in a place of this size. Modern plumbing and electricity would be rare to find in these houses.

Picture 22 – These photos are of some unexploded ordinance that locals asked us to secure. We secured the area where these and other unexploded ordinance was lying until the explosive ordnance disposal (EOD) team could arrive and dispose of it safely.

Picture 23 – This photo is of a pushcart owned by one of the travelers crossing the Pakistani border into Afghanistan. He tried to smuggle the pistol inside his cart and used the plants to conceal it from our view as he walked by. Inside the bags were several boxes of ammunition. The traveler and our findings got turned over to the local Afghan National Directorate of Security (NDS) officers. The NDS is roughly the equivalent of the American Department of Homeland Security.

Picture 24 - Part of our mission was to train Afghan Army soldiers and Afghan Border Police (ABP) officers. Here you can see several ABP officers participating in training to detain a suspect. A few months after I returned home, an ABP officer who joined the Taliban killed six US Army soldiers during a training exercise like this. We always had several armed soldiers present during our training to prevent those types of attacks.

Picture 25 - This picture shows the Battlefield Crosses for Steven DeLuzio and Tristan Southworth. Both Steven and Tristan died during the same mission on August 22, 2010. Each Battlefield Cross consists of the soldier's helmet, rifle, dog tags, and boots, along with a picture of the soldier. Battlefield Crosses serve as a memorial and are displayed to honor and respect the fallen soldiers. Attending the funeral is not always possible for soldiers who are still in combat.

Picture 26 - This photo shows the wall of stickers left by travelers in Leipzig, Germany. The VT oval sticker and ski resort sticker that I noticed are to the right of the "no smoking" sticker in the center.

Picture 27 – An Army carry team brings the transfer case containing Steven's remains past Admiral Mike Mullen on Tuesday, Aug. 24, 2010, at Dover Air Force Base. Admiral Mullen was the 17th Chairman of the Joint Chiefs of Staff, who you can see on the far right side of this photo, saluting Steven as the transfer case gets carried off of the plane. (U.S. Air Force photo/Roland Balik)

Picture 28 – This bugler plays Taps at Steven's funeral with several Patriot Guard Riders standing in the background. Taps is a bugle call that is traditionally played at military funerals by a single bugler. ©Brian Ambrose, 2010

Picture 29 - A three-volley salute, sometimes referred to as a 21-gun salute, is a ceremonial act performed at military funerals. The honor guard, consisting of seven members, fires three shots into the air. The rounds they fire are blanks for safety purposes, so no bullets leave the guns, yet they still make a loud sound like they were using live ammunition. ©Brian Ambrose, 2010

Picture 30 – In and around 2010, the Westboro Baptist Church would frequently attend the funerals of fallen soldiers to protest the war as part of their "Thank God for Dead Soldiers" campaign. The Patriot Guard Riders formed a human wall and carried large American flags to keep them away from us if they showed up. Fortunately, the WBC didn't attend Steven's funeral. ©Brian Ambrose, 2010

Picture 31 – A barracks building on Bagram Air Base was named DeLuzio Hall in Steven's memory. This photo is the plaque placed outside the entrance to the building.

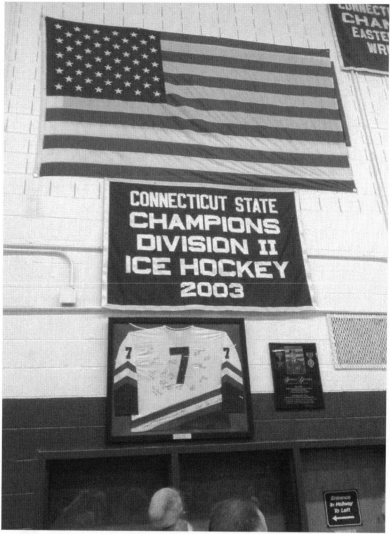

Picture 32 – Our high school retired Steven's hockey number 7 after his death. Steven's favorite hockey player, Ray Bourque of the Boston Bruins, wore number 7 until it was retired for Phil Esposito. Bourque took off his number 7 jersey during the retirement ceremony and handed it to Esposito, revealing a second jersey that he was wearing underneath with his permanent number 77. When Steven's number 7 was retired, the student who wore number 7 that year took his jersey off and handed it to us, revealing his number 77 jersey underneath. It was quite a fitting tribute. I'm sure Steven was smiling down at the ceremony that day.

Picture 33 - This photo is one of the many television, radio, and newspaper interviews I gave in the months following Steven's death. This photo shows me talking to a local television reporter at the first memorial golf tournament. We held it at the same country club that we had the reception after Steven's funeral.

Picture 34 – It took us about five years after moving to Arizona for my wife, kids, and me to make it to the Grand Canyon.

Picture 35 – My parents and I got a private tour of the West Wing the night before the Gold Star Family event at The White House. The West Wing is not typically a part of the public tours. We weren't allowed to take any pictures inside the West Wing except in the Press Briefing Room. We toured the Oval Office, Roosevelt Room, Cabinet Room, Navy Mess and Ward Room, the Rose Garden, and the Situation Room. To be clear, we only saw the door to the Situation Room. During our visits to The White House, we encountered many Secret Service agents who were extremely polite and friendly despite Hollywood's portrayal.

Picture 36 – During the Gold Star Family event at The White House, we were allowed access to some of the rooms in the East Wing. Many of which had items from other Presidents throughout our country's history. This picture includes a plate and sauce boat purchased by President George Washington between 1789 and 1797.

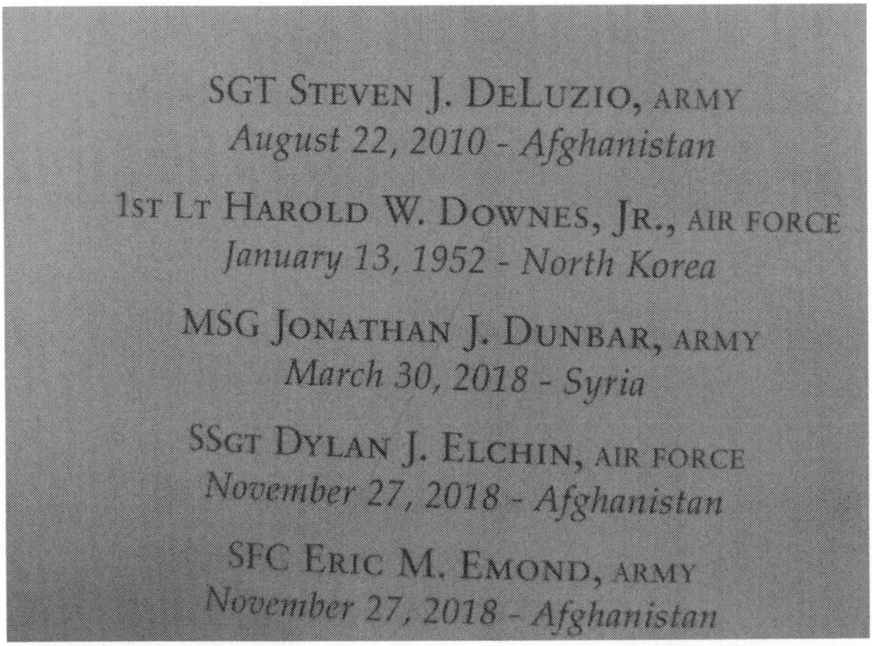

SGT STEVEN J. DELUZIO, ARMY
August 22, 2010 - Afghanistan

1ST LT HAROLD W. DOWNES, JR., AIR FORCE
January 13, 1952 - North Korea

MSG JONATHAN J. DUNBAR, ARMY
March 30, 2018 - Syria

SSGT DYLAN J. ELCHIN, AIR FORCE
November 27, 2018 - Afghanistan

SFC ERIC M. EMOND, ARMY
November 27, 2018 - Afghanistan

Picture 37 – This photo includes part of the program at the Gold Star Family event at The White House, including Steven's name.

Picture 38 – This photo includes my parents (right) and I (left) with President Donald Trump and First Lady Melania Trump in the Blue Room of The White House during a May 2019 Gold Star Family event. Before entering the room, a naval officer told us not to have anything in our hands as we got introduced to the President. I had Steven's challenge coin, which I presented to the President in the traditional handshake method. I don't follow the rules all that well, I guess! Fortunately, I did not get tackled by Secret Service agents.

Resources

Here are some resources for veterans and Gold Star families that I would like to share.

22 Until None

https://www.22untilnone.org/

1-866-254-9961

* * *

American Gold Star Mothers

https://www.goldstarmoms.com/

* * *

Children of Fallen Soldiers Relief Fund

https://www.cfsrf.org/

* * *

Drive On Podcast Resources

https://driveonpodcast.com/resources-for-veterans-and-their-families/

* * *

Folds of Honor

https://www.foldsofhonor.org/

* * *

Gold Star Awareness
https://www.goldstarawareness.com/

* * *

Gold Star Wives of America, Inc.
https://www.goldstarwives.org/

* * *

National Association of State Directors of Veterans
https://www.nasdva.us/

* * *

National Association of County Veterans Service Officers
https://www.nacvso.org/

* * *

Stop Soldier Suicide
https://stopsoldiersuicide.org/

* * *

The Society of Military Widows
http://www.militarywidows.org/

* * *

Tragedy Assistance Program for Survivors (TAPS)

https://www.taps.org/

* * *

U.S. Army Survivor Outreach Services
1-855 707-2769

* * *

U.S Navy Gold Star Program
1-888-509-8759

* * *

Vet Center
https://www.vetcenter.va.gov/

Glossary

- 21-gun salute: A customary gun salute performed by firing guns, cannons, or artillery as a military honor.
- 30th Adjutant General (30th AG): The unit responsible for preparing recruits for infantry training.
- Afghan Border Police (ABP): A police force that secures Afghanistan's border with neighboring countries.
- ACOG: Advanced Combat Optical Gunsight. This scope provides 4x magnification to improve the visibility of distant targets.
- Agent Orange: Agent Orange is a tactical herbicide used by the US military to clear foliage during the Vietnam War. Many US service members have been diagnosed with various forms of cancer after their exposure to Agent Orange.
- Air Assault: The movement of ground forces by helicopters.
- AIT: Advanced Individual Training
- AK-47: A gas-operated rifle chambered to fire the 7.62x39mm cartridge.
- Annual Training: The yearly training period, which typically lasts for two weeks. The purpose is to improve soldiers' skills with extended military training they would not ordinarily get on a two or three-day weekend training.
- Army Combat Uniform (ACU): This is the duty uniform worn by soldiers between 2004 and 2019. It featured a digital camouflage pattern, which many soldiers felt did not adequately blend in with their surroundings.
- ASVAB: Armed Services Vocational Aptitude Battery. It is a multiple-choice test given to determine a prospective service member's qualification for entering military service.

- AT-4: An unguided, single-shot, 84mm anti-tank weapon.
- AWOL: Absent Without Leave. The term to describe a service member who has left their post without permission.
- Barracks: Barracks are military housing, with many bunk beds with 30+ soldiers in one room.
- Battalion: Battalions are Army units consisting of a headquarters company and at least two other companies. Typically battalions have anywhere between 400-1,200 soldiers assigned to them. A Lieutenant Colonel commands them.
- Battlefield Cross: A memorial tribute to a fallen soldier. The battlefield cross includes the soldier's boots, bayonet, rifle, helmet, and dog tags.
- Bazaar: An outdoor market with Afghan vendors selling various products, including clothing, rugs, knock-off sunglasses and jewelry, and bootleg videos.
- Blouse: The uniform's outer top. Typically this has a soldier's rank, name, unit patches, and awards or badges attached.
- Brigade: An Army unit consisting of three to six battalions. Brigades typically have anywhere between 2,000-8,000 soldiers assigned to them.
- Brigade Commander: The Brigadier General (one star) or Colonel assigned to command a Brigade.
- Burn Pits: Refers to an area on a FOB where garbage and other waste gets burned. Frequently these burn pits would contain plastics, electronics, and biohazardous materials. Service members on these bases would often breathe in the fumes from these burn pits.
- C-17: A large military transport aircraft, which delivers troops and cargo throughout the world.
- C-4: A plastic explosive, which uses RDX as its explosive agent. It has a texture similar to modeling clay.
- Casualty Assistance Officer: Soldiers responsible for notifying a service member's family in the event of their death. They may also assist in making funeral arrangements or submit claims to government agencies for benefits on behalf of families.
- CH-47 Chinook: A twin-engine, dual-rotor helicopter. A wide loading

ramp at the helicopter's rear allows troops and cargo to load on and off quickly. Each can hold up to 55 passengers.

- Challenge Coin: Are presented to troops to instill pride or represent a unit. They often are given to dignitaries as a sign of respect. Military members will give a coin to a subordinate for recognition.
- Chow Hall: Army slang for an on-base dining facility.
- Class A Dress Uniform: Refers to the green dress uniform that soldiers wore between 1954 and 2015.
- CO: Commanding Officer. The officer in command of a military unit.
- Company: A company is an Army unit consisting of two to four platoons. Companies typically have anywhere between 100-250 soldiers assigned to them. A Captain commands a company.
- Cover: The hat worn by soldiers.
- CS Gas: CS is also known as tear gas. CS is a gas typically used in riot control, as exposure to it causes eyes to burn and tear up. It also irritates the nose, mouth, and throat, which causes anyone exposed to cough and have difficulty breathing.
- DFAC: See Chow Hall.
- EOD: Explosive Ordnance Disposal.
- First Sergeant: Is a senior non-commissioned officer. They are the highest-ranking enlisted soldier in a company.
- FOB: Forward Operating Base. A FOB is a military base used to support military activities in an area. A FOB enables troops to get distributed across a wide area versus having them all on one central base.
- Formation: An arrangement of troops, organized in orderly columns and rows.
- FTX: Field Training Exercise. A military exercise where a unit conducts tactical operations in simulated combat conditions.
- Gold Star Family: The title given to families of military members who died in service to their country. Often used interchangeably with the family member's relationship to the deceased (Gold Star Mother, Father, Brother, Sister, etc.)
- Grog: Grog is a mix of Gatorade, water, and dry ice. There are rumors

that the grog mixture contains alcohol. It does not.

- HESCO Barrier: A collapsible wire mesh container with a heavy fabric liner. The container is filled with local dirt and rocks to form a wall around a FOB or other military installations. Often these are stacked at least two high and even several deep to create a more secure barrier.

- HMMWV: High Mobility Multi-Wheeled Vehicle. Also referred to as a "Humvee" or "hummer." It is a four-wheeled military vehicle with hardened or soft sides and a roof-mounted turret for a machine gunner's use.

- Honor Guard: Military guards assigned to accompany a casket at a military funeral.

- Infantry Blue Cord: A blue cord is an Army decoration worn on the right shoulder of qualified infantrymen. It is light blue and worn with the soldier's dress uniform.

- Infantry Crossed Rifles: The insignia of the US Army infantry. It consists of two 1795 Springfield muskets crossed over each other.

- IRR: Inactive Ready Reserve. It consists of trained soldiers who have previously served in the Army and met their military contract obligations.

- Jingle Truck: Ornately decorated trucks. Colorful paintings adorn the truck's exterior, and often bells are strung on the truck's bumper (hence the name "jingle" truck). Some truck drivers will spend two years' salary on decorating their trucks.

- JRTC: Joint Readiness Training Center. Located at Ft. Polk, Louisiana, JRTC focuses on improving unit readiness by providing realistic training to prepare for combat.

- M-16: A 5.56mm rifle, which initially entered into military service during the Vietnam War. It is capable of semi-automatic or three-round burst fire.

- M-2: A heavy machine gun designed to fire the .50 BMG round, known as "Ma Deuce" by soldiers. Ma Deuce refers to the M-2 nomenclature. It can be fired from a tripod or mounted to a vehicle.

- M-203: A single-shot 40mm grenade launcher designed to attach under a rifle's barrel.

- M-240B: A belt-fed, gas-operated machine gun that fires the 7.62x51mm round. It can be fired from a bipod, tripod, or mounted to a vehicle.
- M-249 SAW: Squad Automatic Weapon
- M-4: Similar to the M-16. It has a shorter barrel length for a more lightweight and easier to maneuver rifle.
- M-500 Shotgun: Mossberg 500 pump-action shotgun that fires 12 gauge rounds.
- M-67: A fragmentation hand grenade, consisting of a round steel body filled with composition B explosives. It uses a delay fuse, which detonates 4-5 seconds after activation. The steel body fragments and creates a fatality radius of 5 meters and can injure 15 meters away.
- MEPS: Military Entrance Processing Station. These stations ensure applicants are eligible for military service by administering various medical examinations, background checks, and ASVAB tests.
- MOUT: Military Operations in Urban Terrain. Refers to military operations that are conducted in towns and cities rather than out in the open. The presence of civilians usually complicates it. Some combatants may be tough to distinguish from ordinary civilians as they do not often wear uniforms.
- MRAP: Mine-Resistant Ambush Protected. A term for tactical vehicles designed to deflect IED attacks. It deflects the blast from IEDs with its armored V-shaped hull. These vehicles had a higher center of gravity. They were more prone to rollovers on the poor road conditions in Afghanistan.
- MRE: Meals Ready to Eat. Military field rations designed for consumption in combat or other situations where traditional dining facilities were not available. They are known not to be very tasty and have earned nicknames such as "Meals Rejected by Everyone" or "Meals Refusing to Exit."
- MWR: Morale, Welfare, and Recreation. MWR is an organization that provides free and discounted recreation to service members and their families.
- Name Tape: An embroidered piece of fabric containing a service member's last name. Service members wear them on the right breast of their

duty uniform.

- National Guard: A military reserve component under the control of both the state and the federal government. The National Guard consists of Army and Air Force components. Most National Guard service members hold a civilian job while serving part-time in their military unit.
- NATO: North Atlantic Treaty Organization. NATO is a military alliance consisting of 30 countries. Each country agrees to defend the other country if one of them comes under attack.
- NDS: Afghan National Directorate of Security. The national intelligence and security forces of Afghanistan. It is roughly equivalent to the US Department of Homeland Security.
- OCS: Officer Candidate School. An Army school that trains potential commissioned officers of the US Army.
- Order Arms Command: It is a drill and ceremony command given after rendering a salute. It instructs the formation to lower their arms to their normal position by their side.
- Patriot Guard Riders: Members attend military funerals, form honor guards, and protect mourning family members from protesters or other forms of harassment. They will also participate in funerals of veterans who do not have a family.
- PKM: A gas-operated, air-cooled, belt-fed machine gun that fires from an open bolt.
- Platoon: An Army unit consisting of three to four squads. Platoons typically have anywhere between 20-50 soldiers assigned to them. A Lieutenant commands them.
- Platoon Leader: The soldier in charge of a platoon. Typically a junior officer, such as a Second Lieutenant or First Lieutenant.
- Platoon Sergeant: The senior enlisted member of a platoon who provides advice to the platoon leader. A Sergeant First Class typically holds this position.
- Podcast: A series of digital audio files that listeners can listen to on a computer or mobile device.
- PX: Post Exchange. A retail store found on Army bases.

- POTUS: President of the United States
- Pro-Mask: A protective mask designed to protect the wearer from inhaling toxic fumes. It forms a tight seal over the wearer's face. It contains a filter to remove any contaminants from the air that the wearer is breathing.
- PT: Physical Training.
- PTSD: Post Traumatic Stress Disorder. PTSD is a mental disorder that develops due to exposure to a traumatic event. While this disorder is commonly associated with combat veterans, traumatic events such as assaults and traffic accidents can bring about PTSD symptoms.
- QRF: Quick Reaction Force. A military unit that can rapidly respond to support other units.
- Rack: Refers to a bed. It may be an actual bed, a cot, or something similar. Soldiers will "rack out," meaning they are going to sleep.
- Ramadan: Ramadan is the month-long observation of fasting, prayer, and other reflections by Muslims.
- ROTC: Reserve Officers' Training Corps. It is a college-based officer training program used to train commissioned officers. Students attend college classes like other students and receive military training through a unit near the college. The ROTC originated at Norwich University in Northfield, Vermont.
- RPG: Rocket Propelled Grenade. RPGs are shoulder-fired weapons that launch grenades attached to a rocket that propels the grenade towards its target.
- Sensitive Items: A piece of equipment that is either harmful or expensive. Items such as weapons, night vision goggles, weapon sights, etc., are considered sensitive items.
- Sergeant Major: Sergeants major are senior non-commissioned officers and the highest enlisted rank. At the battalion level, the Sergeant Major serves as the senior enlisted advisor to the battalion commander.
- Squad: A squad is an Army unit consisting of two teams. Squads typically have approximately nine soldiers assigned to them split into two teams. A Staff Sergeant leads them.

- Surviving Sons and Daughters: Found in Army Regulation 635-200 Active Duty Enlisted Administrative Separations. It specifies that any son or daughter in a family whose parent or one or more sons or daughters killed in action may get separated from the Army.
- Taps: A bugle call played at military funerals by a single bugler.
- Team: The smallest Army unit besides an individual soldier. Two teams make up a squad referred to as "Alpha" and "Bravo" teams. Each team gets led by a Sergeant and contains three other soldiers - a grenadier, a machine gunner, and a rifleman.
- Three-Volley Salute: See 21-gun salute.
- TOC: Tactical Operations Center. A command post where several soldiers will help coordinate troops on the ground and other supporting elements such as medevacs, artillery, or air support.
- Torkham Border Crossing: Torkham is a major border crossing between Afghanistan and Pakistan. It connects Afghanistan's Nangahar province to Pakistan's Khyber Pakhtunkhwa province. The road that passes through it connects Islamabad in Pakistan to Kabul in Afghanistan. Goods transported through Torkham arrive at the port in Karachi, Pakistan, and get moved by truck through Torkham. Approximately 80% of NATO supplies pass through Torkham.
- Transfer Case: A rectangular metal case similar in size to a casket. It contains the remains of fallen US service members. They are draped with an American flag to honor the sacrifice of the service member.
- TC: Truck Commander. Usually sits in the front passenger seat and is in charge of everything in the assigned vehicle.
- Turning Blue Ceremony: A ceremony held the day before graduation from US Army Infantry Advanced Individual Training. New infantry soldiers get presented with the blue cord, which is authorized to be worn only by infantry-qualified soldiers.
- VA: Department of Veteran's Affairs. Provides services to veterans to support them after their time in service. It provides physical and mental health services, housing assistance, administers disability and pension benefits, and other related services.

- Vet Center: Counseling centers that provide a range of social and psychological services. It offers individual, group, and family counseling services and helps work through the trauma families and soldiers experience during the war.
- Wadi: A valley, gully, or streambed that is dry except during the rainy season.
- Westboro Baptist Church: WBC is an American hate group not affiliated with the Baptist church. They are known for protesting military funerals holding signs that say "Thank God for dead soldiers," and other inflammatory statements.

Index

- 1/102nd Infantry, 46
- 100 Brilliant Companies To Watch, 92
- 21-Gun Salute, 86
- 3/172 Infantry, 7, 60
- 3rd Platoon, 60
- 4S's, 45
- 9/11, 1, 13, 130, 131
- A Company 3/172 Infantry Regiment, 7, 60
- ABP, 60, 63, 64, 154
- Absent Without Leave, *See AWOL*
- Accident, 10, 11, 12,
- Accounting, 6, 11, 13, 17, 18
- ACOG, 45
- ACU, 22, 77
- Advanced Combat Optical Gunsight, *See ACOG*
- Advanced Individual Training, *See AIT*
- Afghan Border Patrol, *See ABP*
- Agent Orange, 141
- Air Assault, 54, 56
- Air Force, 15, 19, 89, 157
- AIT, 8, 15, 27, 86
- AK-47, 44, 61
- Al Anbar Province, 9
- Ali Al Salem Air Base, 72
- Alpha Company, 60

- Ambush, 47, 56, 60, 61, 63, 78
- American, 1-5, 14, 49, 52, 58, 63-67, 73, 84, 128-130, 143, 146, 153, 160
- Amnesty Room, 20, 21
- Anxiety, 59, 105, 128
- AO, 46
- AR 670-1, 50
- Area of Operations, *See AO*
- Arizona, 104-106, 112, 113, 164
- Arlington, 119
- Armed Services Vocational Aptitude Battery, *See ASVAB*
- Army Combat Uniform, *See ACU*
- Army National Guard, 7, 15, 18, 79, 88, 96
- Army Regulations, 97
- Art, 122, 123
- ASVAB, 15, 16
- AT-4, 25
- Atlanta, 19, 31, 36, 76, 78, 104
- Autopsy, 71, 81, 82
- AWOL, 27
- Bagram, 42, 64, 68, 71, 75, 124, 161
- Barracks, 15, 18, 20-28, 37, 39, 42
- Barrier, 66, 83
- Baseball, 2, 4, 23, 82, 84
- Basketball, 5, 41
- Battalion, 17, 59
- Battle Fatigue, 2
- Battlefield Cross, 155
- Bazaar, 145
- Birthday, 2, 14, 15, 24, 90, 104
- Black, Wes, 61, 62, 121
- Blood, 3, 10, 29, 30, 60, 62, 63
- Blouse, 70, 72
- Blue Cord, 30, 31, 133

- Blue Man Group, 90
- Blue Room, 120, 168
- Body Armor, 81, 110, 128
- Body Bags, 2
- Border Crossing, 43, 44, 46
- Boston Bruins, 4, 5, 162
- Bourque, Ray, 106, 162
- Brigade, 69
- Brigade Commander, 59, 70, 89
- British Indian, 43
- Bryant College, 11
- Buddy Carries, 55
- Burn Pits, 121, 122, 141
- C-17, 72
- Cabinet Room, 118, 165
- Cadet of the Month, 9
- Caffeine, 110
- Camp Atterbury, 35-39, 88-90, 134, 135
- Camp Shelby, 10
- Cantor, 85
- Career Aptitude Test, 11
- Casket, 71, 81-83
- Casualty Assistance Officer, 82
- Casualty Collection point, *see CCP*
- Cattle, 19-23
- CCP, 63, 64
- CDC, 35
- Cemetery, 82, 86, 87, 119
- CH-47, 56
- Chain of Command, 35, 41, 97
- Challenge Coin, 120
- Chaplain, 69
- Charlie Company, 46, 64

- Checkpoint, 19, 44
- Chemotherapy, 121, 122, 125, 131
- Chink in your Armor, 39
- Chinook, *See CH-47*
- Chow Hall, *See DFAC*
- Christening, 38, 136
- Church, 38, 82, 84, 85, 86
- CIA, 52
- Civilian Life, 88, 102
- Class A Dress Uniform, 82
- Class President, 6
- CNN, 12
- CO (Commanding Officer), 28
- Co-Captain, 6
- Coach, 2, 6, 84, 85
- Coffee, 18, 92, 104, 109, 110
- Cold War, 3
- College, 6, 7, 11, 13, 14, 16, 18, 22, 32, 49, 93
- Combat Outpost, *See COP*
- Combat Zone, 10, 75, 102, 128
- Communication, 57, 70, 99, 100
- Communication Blackout, 70
- Connecticut Army National Guard, 15, 88
- COP, 60, 61, 64
- Corps of Cadets, 6
- Couch, Dick, 31
- Counseling, 111-113
- Country Club, 87, 163
- Cover, 72
- Cross Rifles, 29, 30
- Crusader-Six, 58
- CS Gas, 25
- Death, iv, vi, 70-77, 79-87, 92, 93, 101-112, 121, 130, 162, 163

- DeLuzio, Adam, 101–103, 106, 136
- DeLuzio, Alfred, 1, 13, 124
- DeLuzio, Charlotte, 103, 106
- DeLuzio, Diane (Mom), 2, 4, 8, 10, 13, 14, 78, 79, 90, 106, 120, 131
- DeLuzio, Mark (Dad), 2, 3, 5, 10, 12, 13, 28, 32, 36, 79, 90–93, 106, 117
- DeLuzio, Raymond, 103–106
- DeLuzio, Victoria, 33–38, 73, 74, 77, 78, 95, 99–103, 106, 107, 110, 116, 136, 195
- Department of Veteran's Affairs, *See VA*
- Depression, 116, 124
- Depressive Disorder, 114
- DFAC, 42
- Director of Operations, 91
- DOD, 48, 50
- Dog River Run, 7
- Dog Tags, 22, 36, 155
- Dover Air Force Base, 71, 81, 157
- Dream, 2, 30, 91, 92
- Drill Sergeant, 8, 13, 14, 20–30
- Drinking, 54, 90, 92, 104, 109, 125
- Drive On Podcast, 121–123, 125, 126, 127, 195
- Durand Line, 43
- E-Tool, 23
- East Wing, 119, 166
- Elevation, 55
- Emergency Room, 3
- Energy Drinks, 110, 111
- Entrepreneur Magazine, 92
- EOD, 47, 57, 81, 152
- Equine-Assisted Therapy, 122
- ESPN, 5
- Eulogy, 85
- Explosive Ordnance Disposal, *See EOD*

- FAA, 12
- FBI, 11–13
- Field Training Exercise, *See FTX*
- Firefighter, 84, 122
- First Sergeant, 29, 31
- "Floor You Can't Walk On," 94
- FOB, 42, 43, 46, 49–55, 140, 141, 147, 149
- Footbridge, 40
- Formation, 22, 29, 30
- Forward Operating Base, *See FOB*
- French Soldiers, 58
- Ft. Benning, 8, 11, 17, 19–23
- Ft. Dix, 34
- FTX, 27, 29
- Funeral, 82–88, 155, 158, 159, 160, 163
- Gas Masks, 25
- Germany, 1, 41, 42, 75, 76, 139, 156
- Glastonbury, 83, 86
- Global War on Terror, 128
- Gold Star, 165–168
- Golden Treasure, 29
- Golf, 2, 4, 5, 87, 113, 149, 164
- Gomer Pyle, 22
- Grenade, 25, 41, 47, 61, 63, 67, 68, 81
- Grief, 73, 75, 77, 81, 94, 102, 112
- Grog, 29
- Gulf War, 4
- Gutt, Leeza, 8, 14, 15, 27, 38, 74, 103, 136
- H1N1, 34, 36
- Hadyka, Joanne (Aunt Joanne), 77, 79
- Hadyka, Kevin, 85
- Hadyka, Michael, 83
- Hadyka, Phil (Uncle Phil), 77, 78

- Happy Little Trees, 122
- "Head on a Swivel," 128
- Helicopter, 42, 43, 54, 56-60, 63, 64, 67-70, 75, 96
- Herrera, 60, 61, 64
- HESCO Barrier, 44
- HMMWV, *See Humvee*
- Hockey, 4-7, 85, 106, 162
- Hofstra University, 6
- Holy Cross Cemetery, 86
- Homeland Security, 45, 153
- Honor Guard, 83, 84, 159
- Honor Hill, 29
- Humvee, 39, 40, 138
- Hurricane Sandy, 104
- "I Will Never Leave A Fallen Comrade," 63, 69, 80, 84
- ICU, 35
- IED, 32
- Inactive Ready Reserve, *See IRR*
- Indiana, 35, 37, 38, 83, 88, 89, 137
- Infantry, 7-9, 16, 25, 29-31, 46, 52, 86, 127, 133
- International Security Assistance Force, *See ISAF*
- Interpreter, 45, 54, 67, 112, 128
- Iraq, 7, 9, 10, 18, 27, 31-32, 38, 57, 122, 133
- IRR, 14, 96
- ISAF, 53
- Iwo Jima, 1
- Jackson, Hallie, 79
- Jaji, 61
- JFK, 119
- Jingle Truck, 44, 114, 142
- Joint Readiness Training, 39
- JRTC, 39
- Kevlar, 23, 55

- Khyber Rifles, 146
- KIA, 105
- Knock at the Door, 70
- Korean War, 30
- Kuwait, 64, 69–76, 80, 84, 93
- Kyrgyzstan, 42
- Labor, 35, 59
- Jalalabad, 42, 47
- Landing Zone, *See LZ*
- Las Vegas, 52, 90
- License Plates, 143
- Life of a Cadet, 7
- Lock your Knees, 29
- "Loose Lips Sink Ships," 73, 78
- Louisiana, 39
- Lysik, Joseph, 1, 2, 59
- LZ, 63, 64
- M-16, 23, 25
- M-2, 25
- M-203, 25
- M-240B, 25, 55
- M-249 SAW, 25
- M-67, 25
- M-203 Grenade Launcher, 25
- M-4, 41, 68
- M-500, 68
- Ma Deuce, 25
- Machine Gun, 25, 40, 44, 55, 61, 62, 67
- Man-Jams, 51
- Manchester, CT, 15
- Meals Ready to Eat, *See MRE*
- Medic, 41, 46, 62, 63
- Mehtar Lam, 49

- Memorial Day, 28, 117
- Memorial Service, 71
- Memory, 37, 79, 114, 116, 117, 120, 161
- Mental Health, 92, 113, 125, 126, 128
- MEPS, 15, 16, 18, 19
- Military Entrance Processing Station, *See MEPS*
- Military Operations In Urban Terrain, *See MOUT*
- Mine-Resistant Ambush Protected, *See MRAP*
- Montreal Canadiens, 4
- Morale, 30, 38, 113
- Mortician, 81, 82
- Mortuary Affairs Team, 81, 82
- Mountain Climbing, 122
- MOUT, 37
- MRAP, 56
- MRE, 26, 27
- Mullen, Mike Admiral, 157
- Murphy, Audie, 48, 49
- Music, 30, 85, 122, 124
- Muslim, 53, 54
- "My Side," 32
- Name Tape, 78
- National Anthem, 4
- NATO, 46, 53
- Navy Seal, 31
- Nazi, 1
- NCO, 48, 49, 67
- NDS, 45, 153
- Newton, Robert (Uncle Bob), 30
- Night Vision Goggles, 54, 57, 58, 64
- Night Vision Lens, 4
- Non-Deployable Status, 9
- Norfolk, VA, 118

- Norwich University, 6-10, 31, 69
- Nutt, Chaplain, 74, 97
- Obituary, 82
- OCS, 16
- Officer Candidate School, *See OCS*
- Operation Desert Storm, 4
- Order Arms, 72
- Oval Office, 118, 120, 165
- Painting, 119, 122-124
- Pakistan, 43, 44, 46, 50, 51, 86, 115, 144, 146, 147, 154
- Paktia, 61
- Pashto, 66
- Patriot Guard Riders, 86, 158, 160
- Pentagon, 12
- Personal Security Detachment, 50
- Philippines, 1
- Photography, 122
- Physical Training, *See PT*
- PKM, 61, 62
- Platoon, 24, 26, 29, 30, 39, 40, 46, 47, 48, 49, 50, 55, 60, 61-67, 91, 97, 127, 138
- Platoon Leader, 39, 48
- Platoon Sergeant, 48, 52, 57, 58, 97
- Pledge of Allegiance, 4
- Podcast, 121-127
- Poland, 1
- Pole-less Litter, 63
- Politicians, 86
- Post Exchange, *See PX*
- Post-Traumatic Stress Disorder, *See PTSD*
- Press Briefing Room, 118, 119, 165
- Private, 6, 22, 24, 25, 40, 97
- Pro-Mask, 25

- PSD, 50, 51
- PT, 7-9, 21
- PTSD, 2, 114, 116, 122, 124-128
- Pushcart, 153
- PX, 21
- QRF, 47, 48
- Quick Reaction Force, *See QRF*
- Rack, 39, 120
- Ramadan, 53
- Ramadi, 9, 31, 32, 57
- Ramp Ceremony, 71, 93
- Rappel Tower, 28, 30
- Red Cross, 35, 59, 85
- Rifle, 23, 25, 29, 30, 37, 41, 45, 49, 65, 68, 115, 128, 142, 146, 155
- Rock Bottom Moment, 110
- Rocket Propelled Grenade, *See RPG*
- Rook, 6, 7, 9
- Roosevelt Room, 118, 165
- Roqian, 61
- Rose Garden, 118, 165
- Ross, Bob, 122
- ROTC, 6
- Roxy, 73, 95
- RPG, 47, 63, 65, 68
- Santos, Edward, 122, 123
- SAT, 15
- Scar, 3, 82
- Scotty Admin, 91
- Scrapbook, 4
- Sea Level, 55
- Secret Service, 119, 120, 165, 168
- "Secret Squirrels," 52, 53
- Seizures, 107, 116

- Sergeant Major, 31, 41, 59, 69, 70
- Sergeant, 8, 16, 22, 48, 65
- SGTStevenDeLuzio.com, 94
- Shell Shock, 2
- Shotgun, 41, 68
- Situation Room, 118, 165
- Smoked, 23, 24, 29, 67
- Son, 10, 18, 25, 35-38, 49, 59, 65, 71-73, 76-78, 88-97, 99-102, 113, 122, 136
- Southworth, Tristan SGT, 64, 155
- Specialist, 16, 22
- Squad, 25, 39, 48-50, 58, 59, 65-67, 97
- Squad Automatic Weapon (SAW), 25
- State Championship, 6
- State Department, 52, 53
- State Police, 77
- Stitches, 3
- Suicide, 93, 121
- Surgery, 96, 105
- "Surviving Sons and Daughters," 97
- Swine Flu, 34
- TA-50, 23
- Tactical Operations Center, *See TOC*
- Taliban, 46, 47, 52, 53, 56, 57, 60, 94, 130, 131, 154
- Taps, 86, 158
- TC, 39
- Temper, 95
- "The Sheriff of Ramadi," 31, 32
- The Soldier's Creed, 63, 69, 84
- Therapy, 96, 116, 122, 125
- Three-One, 58
- Three-Volley Salute, *See 21-Gun Salute*
- Tijuana, 3, 129

- TOC, 52, 53, 69
- "Top Gun," 3, 85
- Torkham, 42, 43, 46, 51, 55, 140, 141, 149
- Torkham Tours, 51
- Transfer Case, 64, 72, 84, 124, 157
- Transition, 10, 97, 98, 102
- Trauma, 68
- Truck Commander, *See TC*
- Trump, Melania, First Lady, 120, 168
- Trump, Donald, President, 117, 120, 168
- TSA, 36
- Turning Blue, 30, 31, 133
- Uniforms, 4, 6, 21, 22, 30, 50, 53, 57, 70, 84
- United Airlines Flight 93, 12
- US Army General, 58
- US Navy, 1
- USS Boyd, 1
- VA, 96, 111, 116, 122, 125
- Vermont, 6, 9, 10, 37-39, 76
- Vermont National Guard, 7
- Vet Center, 111, 112
- Veteran, 89, 99, 121, 122, 125-130, 141
- Vietnam, 2, 125-130, 141
- VIPs, 48, 51
- Wadi, 147
- Wake, 71, 82, 84, 87
- Warren Buffet's Grandson, 48
- Washington, DC, 118, 119, 166
- Washington, George 119, 166
- *Waterboys*, 19
- WBC, 86, 160
- Welfare, 113
- West Wing, 118, 119, 165

- Westover Air Reserve Base, 4, 9, 15, 18, 132
- Westboro Baptist Church, *See WBC*
- Western Union, 52
- White Armbands, 56
- White House, 117-121, 165-168
- Wooden Gun, 77
- World Trade Center, 12
- WW II, 1, 2, 49, 117
- Yankees, 5, 8
- Yoga, 122
- Zio Haq, 53

About the Author

SCOTT DELUZIO IS AN ARMY VETERAN, having served six years with the Army National Guard, including a deployment to Afghanistan in 2010. Scott's brother, Steven, was also deployed to Afghanistan in 2010. Unfortunately, Steven was killed in action on August 22, 2010. After returning home, Scott struggled with coping with the stresses of combat, the loss of his younger brother, and adjusting back to civilian life. In the years following Scott's deployment, he noticed other veterans dealing with their struggles in unhealthy ways. Scott started his podcast, Drive On Podcast, to connect with current and prior service members. He interviews veterans and civilians to discuss personal triumphs, life experiences, and emotional hardships to give hope and strength to the military community.

Scott lives in Surprise, Arizona, with his wife, Vicki DeLuzio, and their three children.

You can connect with me on:

- ∞ https://survivingsonbook.com
- ∞ https://driveonpodcast.com
- ∞ https://sgtstevendeluzio.com
- ∞ https://instagram.com/driveonpodcast
- ∞ https://instagram.com/scottdeluzio
- ∞ https://twitter.com/driveonpodcast
- ∞ https://twitter.com/scottdeluzio
- ∞ https://facebook.com/driveonpodcast

Subscribe to my newsletter:

- ✉ https://survivingsonbook.com/email

Made in the USA
Middletown, DE
24 October 2021

50934796R00123